The Courtroom as Forum

Modern American Literature

Yoshinobu Hakutani
General Editor

Vol. 1

PETER LANG
New York • Washington, D.C./Baltimore
Bern • Frankfurt am Main • Berlin • Vienna • Paris

Ann M. Algeo

The Courtroom as Forum

Homicide Trials by Dreiser, Wright, Capote, and Mailer

PETER LANG
New York • Washington, D.C./Baltimore
Bern • Frankfurt am Main • Berlin • Vienna • Paris

PS
374
L34
A44
1996

Library of Congress Cataloging-in-Publication Data

Algeo, Ann M.
The courtroom as forum: homicide trials by Dreiser, Wright,
Capote, and Mailer/ Ann M. Algeo.
p. cm. — (Modern American literature; vol. 1)
Includes bibliographical references and index.
1. American fiction—20th century—History and criticism. 2. Law and
literature—United States—History—20th century. 3. Legal stories,
American—History and criticism. 4. Trials (Murder) in literature. 5. Dreiser,
Theodore, 1871–1945. American tragedy. 6. Wright, Richard, 1908–1960.
Native son. 7. Capote, Truman, 1924– . In cold blood. 8. Mailer, Norman.
Executioner's song. I. Title. II. Series: Modern American literature
(New York, N.Y.); vol. 1.
PS374.L34A44   813'.509355—dc20   95-44270
ISBN 0-8204-2733-0
ISSN 1078-0521

Die Deutsche Bibliothek-CIP-Einheitsaufnahme

Algeo, Ann M.:
The courtroom as forum: homicide trials by Dreiser, Wright,
Capote, and Mailer/ Ann M. Algeo. –New York; Washington, D.C./Baltimore;
Bern; Frankfurt am Main; Berlin; Vienna; Paris: Lang.
(Modern American literature; Vol. 1)
ISBN 0-8204-2733-0
NE: GT

Cover design by James F. Brisson.
Cover art by Clevenger Design.

The paper in this book meets the guidelines for permanence and durability
of the Committee on Production Guidelines for Book Longevity
of the Council of Library Resources.

© 1996 Ann M. Algeo.

Printed in the United States of America.

To my parents, for the greatest legacy—
a love of books.

ACKNOWLEDGMENTS

With thanks to Professor James R. Frakes, Lehigh University, of whom it can be said, as Faulkner said of his mentor Phil Stone, he did half the laughing.

With gratitude to my husband, Randy Jones, for his endless supply of cheerful, patient support.

CREDITS

TABLE OF CONTENTS

INTRODUCTION

The attraction of a homicide trial has once again been demonstrated by public interest in the O. J. Simpson trial. We are drawn to the drama that is created by a murder case that features either the plight of a famous defendant, or the commission of an especially brutal crime, or the raising of important social issues in court. When all three of these components are present, as they are in the Simpson case, many of us are fascinated. This appetite for homicide trials reaches back to a time before television cameras could be counted on to provide daily live coverage of events in the courtroom. Before television was the medium for transmitting information about the happenings in court, the written word was the means of describing to an eager public what occurred in a homicide trial.

"Certain crimes seem to epitomize the thinking of their era," notes Meyer Levin in the foreword to his narrative *Compulsion*, based on the 1924 Leopold-Loeb case (xiii). Levin's examples of literary works embodying such crimes are *Crime and Punishment*, arising "out of the feverish soul-searching of the Russia of Dostoevski's period," and *An American Tragedy*, arising "from the sociological thinking of Dreiser's time in America" (xiii). John Hollowell, citing Levin, adds to the list Capote's *In Cold Blood* as exemplifying "the seemingly random, meaningless crime that became symptomatic of America in the sixties" (85). Martin L. Friedland, in his introduction to *Rough Justice: Essays on Crime in Literature*, asserts that studies of crime in literature offer "the insights literature can provide into societal perceptions and representations of crime at the time . . . " as well as reveal "the author's own attitudes toward society and crime" (xii). This study will show that Theodore Dreiser's *An American Tragedy* (1925), Richard Wright's *Native Son* (1940), Truman Capote's *In Cold Blood* (1965), and Norman Mailer's *The Executioner's Song* (1979) comprise a quartet of twentieth-century narratives based on actual crimes that highlight the major social issues of the decades in which the crimes occurred, and that the authors use the courtroom as a forum for the themes that represent the struggle of social forces in each era.

The texts by Dreiser, Wright, Capote, and Mailer were selected for analysis in this book because they are the four works based on actual homicides written by major authors of the century. The publication dates of the texts demonstrate a recurring pattern, approximately every fifteen years, of the need to explore the social and legal issues of each era. Although each writer includes thematic elements distinctive to the age in which he is writing, the works also share the common theme of the outsider in search of the American Dream who seeks justice but has the power of the system used against him in a trial of his guilt or innocence.

The structure of this study is two-tiered. The larger issue, addressed in the introduction and conclusion, is an examination of the contention that certain crimes represent the era in which they occur. Within that broader context, each chapter contains a comparison of an author's trial scene to a model criminal trial, plus an examination of the author's narrative choices and the thematic implications of those choices.

At this point it may be necessary to state what this book is not intended to do. First, this is not a survey of critical theory in the field of law and literature by writers such as Stanley Fish, Richard A. Posner, Richard Weisberg, Robin West, and James Boyd White. The works of these critics are useful and may be cited here, but critical theory is not our focus. In fact, Posner specifically excludes from his text "the description by creative writers of real legal events, such as actual trials" (19). Second, this is not an analysis of the accuracy of the four narratives as "true crime" literature. This study does not pretend to be a survey of the primary materials (transcripts, court files, etc.) of the actual cases on which the narratives are based. For the four works being analyzed here, the actual cases will be discussed only as they serve to highlight the choices made by the authors. Finally, this is not a debate on the merits of literature versus journalism or fiction versus nonfiction for conveying the courtroom experience. That debate will have to occur—or continue—elsewhere. The position held in this study is that *all* descriptions of trial proceedings are fictional whether completely imaginary or based on personal observation, trial transcripts, or newspaper accounts. These texts fall on a continuum from the use of a crime as mere stimulus for the narrative to attempted faithfulness to the trial record. The terms "fiction" and "nonfiction" describe only the opposite ends of the continuum and do not always allow for a productive discussion of works that fall somewhere between. Just as the texts vary as to their use of outside materials, a variety of names have been applied to texts based on actual crimes, including novel, nonfiction novel, "procedural narrative" (Weisberg 226), true crime, fact crime, and "naturalistic atrocity saga" (McWilliams 115). E. L. Doctorow has said, " 'There is no longer any such thing as fiction or nonfiction, there is only narrative' " (qtd. in Fishkin 207). While this statement may be going too far in some circumstances, for example a "made up" story published in a newspaper as fact (Fishkin 210), for purposes of our discussion the term "narrative" will be used.

Authors worldwide have been writing about actual murders for centuries. Although some texts focus only on the commission of the crime, or the psychology of the criminal, or the investigative process, most works include an exploration of the trial process. "The criminal is tried and suffers a severe penalty, with the trial or some equivalent device serving as a forum in which significant issues can be argued and the character's guilt weighed" (Gallagher 167–A). In early twentieth-century America, Edmund Pearson (1880–1937) wrote an account of the 1892 Lizzie Borden case in which Miss Borden was acquitted of the homicide of her father and step-mother. The Borden case, along with narratives on six other cases, including a review of the trials, was published in Pearson's *Studies in Murder* (1924). The introduction to the 1938 Modern Library edition of that work, published posthumously, credits Pearson for founding the school of "criminological literature." The true crime genre was given formal recognition in 1947 when the first "Edgar," named for Poe, was awarded in the category of "fact crime" by the Mystery Writers of America. Although Dreiser and Wright did not initially discuss the relationship between the actual cases on which their texts were based and the finished product, by the 1960s and 70s Capote and Mailer used the true crime basis of their works as an advertising strategy; Capote subtitled *In Cold Blood* "a true account of a multiple murder and its consequences," and *The Executioner's Song* announces on its cover that it is "a true life novel" by Mailer. In a 1966 review of Capote's book, F. W. Dupee wrote, "There is of course a considerable public, generally indulgent, often profitable, for books that reconstruct, whether in a wholly journalistic or a partly 'fictionalized' form, one or another of the more significant criminal episodes of the recent or distant past," and by 1989 Alan Collette noted, "We might be finding ourselves increasingly attracted to forms of literature which *combine* truth and creativity" (Dupee 3; Collette 287).

In the last quarter of the twentieth century there has been an explosion of true crime accounts, most of which include trial scenes. It can be argued that the genre has begun to attract not just more writers but also more talented writers such as Capote and Mailer, and this influx of talent accounts for the increased visibility and acceptability of the genre. It is a matter of both quantity and quality.

The trial usually plays a major role in any narrative based on an actual crime.

> While actual trials do not have the clarity or simplified order of those common to books and plays, they usually involve a discernible conflict centering around a disagreement or criminal act. The individuals involved in the resolution of this conflict voluntarily or involuntarily assume "parts," be it as judge, juror, prosecutor, plaintiff, defendant, or witness, and they act within strict rules that define how they are permitted to behave in the "performance" of justice. Speech is divided into testimony, questioning, cross-examination, and formal argument, all of which take place before an audience. How each participant "performs" can be important, for a judgment can depend not only on what is said but also on the way it is expressed. The good lawyer is a skillful director as well as author, carefully rehearsing his or her presentation and witnesses, even deciding what clothing (perhaps *costume* is the better word) they should wear in court to enhance their case. (Smith 15)

What an author faces when attempting to translate the courtroom experience into words on the page is a daunting task. The writer, just like the lawyer, must make many choices when deciding how to shape a trial in a narrative. In rare cases the author attends the trial, as Capote did, and can supplement the trial transcript with his own impressions of the events as they occur. But being there is not enough. In the courtroom there is a hierarchy of knowledge determined by one's role in the trial. The best-informed person about the trial process is, of course, the judge. Often the judge's law clerk is also privy to the same information as the judge. Best informed about the facts are the attorneys for the prosecution and the defense. The defense attorney may know more because, while the prosecution cannot withhold from the defense any exculpatory evidence discovered during the investigation, reciprocal discovery is not mandatory in all jurisdictions. The defense in some jurisdictions is not required to disclose its strategy unless that strategy includes an alibi or a claim of insanity or mental infirmity. The defendant himself knows the facts but not the technicalities of the trial process. The court personnel know the process but not the facts. The jury knows nothing until opening statements, and each witness knows only his or her small piece of the puzzle. The audience members observing the trial may or may not understand the trial process, depending on their backgrounds—a lawyer visiting the courtroom would automatically understand more about what is going on than most laypeople—but they can only learn the facts as the witnesses testify. Everyone's perception of the events is colored by his or her role in the courtroom. No participant is privy to every point of view.

The limitations of perception are even greater when one is working from a trial transcript rather than personal observation. Most people assume that a transcript is a verbatim record of what happens in the courtroom. However, as Anne Graffam Walker points out in "The Verbatim Record: The Myth and the Reality," all transcripts are edited to a greater or lesser degree. A mistake may be made in recording the words of the speaker or in converting those words into printed form. A court reporter may edit—either consciously or subconsciously—the words of a speaker to make them grammatically correct. But even if there were such a thing as a "perfect" transcript, it would not include all of the elements necessary to recreate the courtroom experience for a reader. A transcript at its best records only words. What a trial transcript cannot account for are elements such as tone of voice; hesitancy or other speech patterns; eye contact; physical characteristics; demeanor or body language including signs of nervousness, composure, laughter, tears; composition and demeanor of the jury; composition of the audience; reactions of the judge, attorneys, defendant, court personnel, jury, and audience to the testimony; and activities in the courtroom "off the record" such as sidebar conferences between the judge and the attorneys or conversations in the audience. The author must supply these missing elements to convey a realistic courtroom experience. An author can describe human reactions; a court reporter is not permitted to do so. With the advent of television cameras in the courtroom, an additional "eye" on the trial process has been provided for a wider audience, and this eye does supply some of the elements missing from a trial transcript.

Even this perspective, however, may produce its own distortion of events based on the placement of the camera, the choices made by the individuals producing the television pictures, and the alleged changes in human behavior based on the mere presence of the camera. McWilliams is correct when he states that only the "fictive record" can "reveal the full complexities, if not the truth, of the issues involved in a trial" (49).

What standard should be applied, then, to determine whether an author has effectively portrayed a courtroom proceeding? Jon L. Breen in the introduction to his bibliography *Novel Verdicts: A Guide to Courtroom Fiction* provides some guidelines, although his work deals with fictional trials, in which group he includes Dreiser's *An American Tragedy* and Meyer Levin's *Compulsion*, and not with texts based on actual cases. Breen cites the following factors for judging "the quality and effectiveness of courtroom scenes": (1) procedural accuracy, (2) fairness to both sides, (3) ingenious points of law and procedure and creative trial tactics, (4) good Q-and-A, and (5) general importance of the trial to the book (x–xi). These factors may be appropriate when examining fictional trials, but narratives based on actual cases must be evaluated in a different manner because the author must deal with certain givens. The questioning in the trial may or may not have been interesting or effective. The lawyers may or may not have used creative trial tactics. The case may or may not have included ingenious points of law or procedure. And although fairness to both sides is the ideal in our system, not all trials are fair. Not only do these givens bind the author to some extent, but the choice of a point of view from which to tell the story may also slant the text in favor of one side or the other. Authors, of necessity, use a selection process to construct trial scenes based on actual cases, and this process is similar to the process lawyers use when they build their cases and construct the sequence of witnesses at trial. James Boyd White views this process as the art of persuading others.

> Whenever he (or she) organizes his material into persuasive form and addresses the audience he wishes to move, the lawyer gives himself a character and establishes, for the moment at least, a relation with his audience, as well as with his client. What kind of character, what kind of community, does he—can he—establish in these ways? What sort of truth, or justice, or beauty, can he be said to serve? (xii–xiii)

Is it not possible to ask the same questions of a writer?

If we accept the premise that the author uses a process of selection to create the trial scene in a narrative, the question becomes what standard should be applied in evaluating whether his choices result in an effective representation of the courtroom experience. We can compare the author's trial scene to the major events of a "model trial," by which we mean a twentieth-century American criminal trial based on common law principles of criminal law and procedure. A model trial would include the following major events: (1) arrest, (2) preliminary arraignment, (3) preliminary hearing or grand jury indictment, (4) arraignment, (5) pretrial motions, (6) jury selection, (7) opening statements, (8) prosecution case-in-chief, (9) defense case-in-chief, (10) prosecution rebuttal witnesses, (11) closing arguments, (12) instructions to the jury, (13) jury deliberations, (14) verdict, (15) sentencing. These events will be described in more detail in the discussion of Theodore Dreiser's *An American Tragedy*, which provides an excellent example of a complete trial in a narrative. As we compare the author's trial scene to the model, we can explore how the writer's narrative choices support his themes which in turn reflect the social issues of the day.

I

Theodore Dreiser's *An American Tragedy*

Theodore Dreiser, introduced to the world of crime as a young reporter in St. Louis, became especially interested in unusual homicide cases. Dreiser collected clippings of these cases as they appeared in the newspapers. He was not alone in his fascination. Murder trials "dominated public attention in the twenties in a way rivaled by no other category of public or private events except sports and the movies" (Brazil 163). Dreiser had for some time considered writing a book about a murderer, and eventually used his collection of unusual homicides to develop "a paradigm of the socially and economically motivated murder" which became the crime at the core of *An American Tragedy* published in 1925 (Plank 269, 284).

An American Tragedy tells the story of Clyde Griffiths from the age of twelve to his execution at twenty-one. The son of poor religious parents who run a street mission, he wants to escape his restrictive environment and takes a job as a bellboy in a hotel, where he learns about the life-style of the rich, about drinking, and about women. One day Clyde is riding with friends and their dates in a borrowed car when they strike and kill a child. Even though he was not driving, Clyde is afraid he will be implicated in the death and runs away. After wandering for two years, he takes a job as a bellboy at the Union League in Chicago, where a chance meeting with his rich uncle, the owner of a collar factory in New York, results in a job offer, and Clyde goes to Lycurgus, New York, to learn his uncle's business. On the job Clyde meets Roberta Alden, who has left the family farm to earn a living in the city. Clyde begins to meet with Roberta outside of work in violation of company policy. At the same time he is drawn into the world of wealth and social status that his uncle's family inhabits. He is invited to dinner at the Griffiths' home and meets the rich Sondra Finchley, a friend of the family. As Clyde begins a physical relationship with Roberta, he is also developing a romantic relationship with Sondra. Clyde falls in love with Sondra and is encouraged by her. He prepares to leave Roberta, but by now she is pregnant. He attempts to obtain an abortion for her, but without money or connections he is unsuccessful. Finally, Roberta demands that he marry her or she will reveal the relationship to their families. Clyde reads a newspaper story about an accidental drowning and considers killing Roberta to escape the situation. He plans a trip for the couple, and they travel under assumed names to a hotel on a lake in the mountains. The couple decides to have a picnic lunch on the lake, and Clyde takes his camera. Once in the rowboat, Roberta, sensing something wrong with Clyde, crawls toward him. As she approaches, Clyde thinks about how he hates himself and her, and he is afraid to act and unable even to speak. Roberta attempts to take the camera from his hand and he lashes out at her, smashing the camera into her face and causing her to fall backward. Clyde rises to reach her—half to assist her, half to apologize—and capsizes the boat, throwing them both into the water. The boat strikes Roberta on the head and she is stunned but manages to yell to Clyde for help. At this point the proverbial voice whispers in Clyde's ear that this was a mishap, that if he tries to rescue her they both might drown as she thrashes about, that if he hesitates a moment she will be gone forever as the result of an accident. As Clyde waits, Roberta sinks from view. Clyde swims to shore, leaving a straw hat behind to convince searchers that he too is dead, buries the camera and tripod in the woods, and hikes to the next town. Once Roberta's body is found, an investigation ensues, and Clyde is arrested, indicted, tried, convicted, and executed for Roberta's murder.

Dreiser described the genesis of *An American Tragedy* in a series of articles published in 1935.[1] As a newspaperman he observed that "almost every young person was possessed of an ingrowing ambition to be somebody financially and socially." "Fortune hunting became a disease" according to Dreiser (qtd. in Saltzman 5, 6). As evidence of this disease Dreiser lists cases of "murder for money" that attracted his attention: Carlyle Harris (1894), Roland Molyneux [Molineux] (1899), Chester Gillette (1906), and Clarence Richesen (1911) (Saltzman 7–8; Lingeman, *Gates* 402; Pizer "*American Tragedy*" 45). Plank argues persuasively that Dreiser did not derive a pattern from the study of these murders as he claimed, but rather he imposed a pattern on crimes only superficially similar in order to support his "paradigm of the socially and economically motivated murder" (269). It is true that Dreiser said it was the psychology of these cases that fascinated him, and he made several aborted attempts to write about a murderer, first Molineux and then Richesen (Saltzman 4; Pizer "*American Tragedy*" 47). He also read the morgue clippings on the William Orpet case and clipped stories on the Gillette case while searching for the "right" murder trial on which to base his narrative (Lingeman, *Journey* 175–76). Barrie Hayne, writing about *An American Tragedy* in *Rough Justice: Essays on Crime in Literature*, tells us that Dreiser rejected a medical student [Carlyle Harris] and a clergyman [Clarence Richesen] as murderers and instead finally chose "the nomadic Chester Gillette" (175).

The most thorough summary of the facts of the Gillette case, based on court records and newspaper stories, has been compiled by John F. Castle in his unpublished dissertation "The Making of *An American Tragedy*" submitted at the University of Michigan in 1952 (14–27). A more concise summary is the entry in *The Murderers' Who's Who*.

GILLETTE, Chester.   American factory worker from humble family
background who wanted to join high society. He worked in his uncle's
garment factory, made steady progress, but had grandiose ideas.

The 22-year-old Gillette's liaison with an 18-year-old secretary, Billie
Brown, at the factory resulted in her pregnancy and she begged Chester to
marry her.

After unsuccessful pleading she threatened to tell Chester's uncle.
Panic-stricken, Chester took her on a hastily arranged holiday, and on 11
July 1906 he rented a boat for a picnic on Big Moose Lake in New York
State. Later Chester was seen drying his clothes by a lakeside bonfire at
Eagle Bay. Billie Brown's body, with the face battered, was washed up the
following day. Chester Gillette, who had inquired at a local hotel whether
there had "been a drowning reported in Big Moose Lake", was arrested.

His trial lasted 22 days, and created considerable public interest. He
said the girl had committed suicide. Then that the boat had capsized and
Billie was drowned accidentally. From his cell Gillette sold autographed
pictures of himself in order to earn money to buy special meals in prison.
Found guilty of murder, he was sentenced to death, and appeals lasted for
a year. Finally he was electrocuted at Auburn prison on 30 March 1908.
Theodore Dreiser based his novel *An American Tragedy* on this case.
(Gaute and Odell 137)

How much of *An American Tragedy* is based on the Gillette case has
always been of interest to critics.[2]   Castle's work contains the most
complete discussion of the issue, including fifty pages of comparisons
between Dreiser's text and the documentary sources (32–82).[3]   It
may be useful, however, to keep in mind Plank's assertion that "this
paradigm of motivation, and not the Gillette case, is for [Dreiser] the
subject of the novel" (286).

Dreiser's material came from a variety of sources: newspaper
accounts of the Gillette trial; discussions of case histories with a
prison psychiatrist, Dr. A. A. Brill; a visit to the Adirondacks to trace
Gillette's journey, to observe the scene of the crime, and to view the
courthouse; interviews while on location with a neighbor of the
victim's family, the rowboat attendant at the lake, and the widow of
the prosecuting attorney; advice from attorneys J. G. Robin and Arthur

Carter Hume; and the work of Clarence Darrow, especially the trial of Leopold and Loeb in 1924 (Lingeman, *Journey* 177, 224–28, 239, 257; Dunlop 387).

There is no agreement over whether Dreiser saw the official transcript of the Gillette trial. He wrote to the District Attorney of Herkimer County, New York, to inquire about the transcript as early as 1920 (Pizer *"American Tragedy"* 49). The "abstract" of the transcript that Castle refers to, not the complete transcript, is made up of 2,109 pages in three volumes (Castle 87). Castle observes that Dreiser would have been able to get several hundred pages of transcribed testimony in Herkimer "just for the asking," but he does not indicate whether Dreiser ever asked. Castle correctly points out that a summary of the trial testimony (which he also calls an "abstract") would have appeared in the published Court of Appeals opinion available at state and law school libraries (12).

Dreiser depended heavily on morgue clippings from the *New York World* newspaper (Castle 32–82; Lingeman *Journey* 227–28). Pizer does an excellent job of delineating what the newspaper provided that the trial transcript could not:

> The account in the *World* summarized such matters [jury selection, medical evidence, minor witnesses] in favor of full coverage of sensational evidence and emotional moments in the trial and much material on such vital concerns for a novelist as Gillette's background, his Cortland love affairs, the atmosphere in the court, the appearance and actions of participants in the trial, and the circumstances of Gillette's execution. . . . The *World*, in short, supplied a good deal of grist for the novelist's mill not available elsewhere and gave this material, by means of emphasis and selection, a kind of preliminary fictional expression which Dreiser had the good sense to recognize as invaluable. (Pizer *"American Tragedy"* 57–58)

Castle says Dreiser transformed all of the documents into a novel by (1) creating a structure of motivation; (2) adding the social background of the 1920s; (3) using the traditions of naturalistic fiction—the element of chance, nature as a conditioning force, frankness about sex; and (4) changing the material by amplification—picking up on hints and suggestions in the documents (98, 119, 129, 135). Examining the material that Dreiser selected to support his themes and seeing how he organized that material for the maximum dramatic impact give us insight into the process of creating an effective trial scene in a narrative.

The themes of *An American Tragedy* include the destructive effects of the American Dream on one who is socially and economically outside the reigning class and the inability of the legal system to deal with such a person and the societal issues he represents. "In this clash of deprived and blessed, not having and having, especially as Dreiser dramatized it, was the stuff of crime, and crime of a kind peculiar to a country where rising through class lines was possible, though fraught with danger—a peculiarly *American* tragedy" (Hayne 170). Dreiser stated his thematic concerns as follows:

> I concluded that there were too many elements of a social and economic, as well as moral and religious, character to permit a jury (themselves the representatives, one might even say the victims, of these same financial conditions and social taboos) to judge fairly the guilt or innocence of the alleged murderer [Gillette]. . . . this was really not an *anti-social* dream as Americans should see it, but rather a *pro-social* dream. *He was really doing the kind of thing which Americans should and would have said was the wise and moral thing for him to do had he not committed a murder.* . . . Not Chester Gillette . . . planned this crime, but circumstances and laws and rules and conventions which to his immature and more or less futile mind were so terrible, so oppressive, that they were destructive to his reasoning powers. (qtd. in Saltzman 9, 10, 12)

Pizer believes Dreiser was expressing "an archetypal American dilemma" (*"American Tragedy"* 45). Lingeman calls it "the American nightmare, a vertiginous fear of falling, of social extinction, of being a nobody" (*Journey* 265). This concept of the outsider with whom the system cannot effectively deal recurs in each of the texts under examination. If anything, the outsiders become more alienated as the century progresses.

An American Tragedy is an excellent example with which to begin our discussion of trial scenes in narratives because it covers the entire trial process from arrest through conviction. Criminal procedure in state courts is governed by state statutes and court rules that can vary from state to state, but the basic principles are similar. To arrest a person for a felony, like homicide, one must have probable cause, that is, evidence that there has been a violation of the law and that the person to be arrested committed the crime. All states allow the police to make a felony arrest without an arrest warrant. The exact pretrial processes and the names of the judicial bodies differ from jurisdiction to jurisdiction, but, in all cases, once the individual is arrested, he [the defendants in our four narratives all happen to be male] will have a preliminary arraignment before a magistrate, usually within 72 hours. The purpose of the preliminary arraignment is to put the defendant on notice of his rights, of the upcoming preliminary hearing, and of the availability of bail if applicable. Usually the accused will be represented by counsel at this stage or will be advised of his right to counsel—a public defender if necessary—at the preliminary arraignment.

Next is either a grand jury hearing or a preliminary hearing before a judge at which evidence is heard to determine probable cause to hold the defendant for trial; if probable cause is found, the grand jury, made up of members of the community, issues an indictment, or the judge has the accused bound over for trial.

The purpose of the next stage, the arraignment, is to formally advise the accused of the charges against him and to allow him to enter his plea of guilty or not guilty. If the plea is not guilty, the accused is held for trial; if the plea is guilty, the accused is scheduled for sentencing. During this pretrial process, plea bargaining may be going on between the prosecutor and the defense attorney. The prosecutor is elected or appointed to represent the state in criminal prosecutions and has a title, such as "district attorney" or "state's attorney," depending on the jurisdiction. In a plea bargain, the prosecutor may offer to lower the charge, from first degree homicide to second degree homicide for example, or to recommend a lenient sentence in exchange for a guilty plea from the defendant that guarantees a conviction and saves the taxpayers an expensive trial.

Prior to trial, the lawyers have the opportunity to file pretrial motions with the judge. These motions may include a motion to exclude evidence, such as a confession; a motion for severance, that is, that two defendants accused of the same crime be tried separately; a motion to suppress evidence that was illegally obtained; a motion for pretrial discovery of the evidence held by the prosecutor; and a motion for a change of venue because a fair trial cannot be held in this particular jurisdiction (Cole 350). Cole cites a Houston defense lawyer who listed the following strategic advantages to aggressive use of pretrial motions:

1. It forces a partial disclosure of the prosecutor's evidence at an early date.
2. It puts pressure on the prosecutor to consider pleabargaining early in the proceeding.
3. It forces exposure of primary state witnesses at an inopportune time for the prosecution.
4. It raises before the trial judge early in the proceedings matters the defense may want called to his or her attention.
5. It forces the prosecutor to make decisions before final preparation of the case.
6. It allows the defendant to see the defense counsel in action, which has a salutary effect on the client-attorney relationship. [note omitted] (350)

Pretrial procedure is described in some detail in *An American Tragedy*. By the time the trial starts, we have covered 126 pages that include the introduction of the district attorney and his investigation; Clyde's arrest and the retention of defense counsel; and the indictment and pretrial motions (Dreiser 503–629). Some of this material reveals the strategies employed by the attorneys and emphasizes the economic and social barriers among the characters.

The District Attorney, Orville Mason, hates Clyde for the wealth and social status he believes Clyde possesses. Hayne argues in addition that "[Mason's] jealousy of Clyde's sexual conquest leads him to prosecute him with more than professional enthusiasm"—an understatement (180). Mason is determined not only to convict Clyde but to use that conviction for his own gain. He asks the governor for a special term of the Supreme Court, the trial-level court in the state of New York, along with a special session of the local grand jury. With these requests granted, Mason is in a position to present evidence to the grand jury, gain an indictment against Clyde, and proceed to trial within four to six weeks, well before the upcoming election in which Mason hopes to become a county judge. He justifies his action by noting the ferocity of public opinion against Clyde:

> And in view of the state of public opinion, which was most bitterly and vigorously anti-Clyde, a quick trial would seem fair and logical to every one in this local world. For why delay? Why permit such a criminal to sit about and speculate on some plan of escape? And especially when his trial by him, Mason, was certain to rebound to his legal and political and social fame the country over. (Dreiser 576–77)

Mason uses the power of his office to gain not justice for Clyde but an advantage for himself. Dreiser included an impending election in his narrative to emphasize the pervasiveness of the corrupting power of the American Dream. (At the time of the actual Gillette trial, the local election had already been held.) Clyde murders to get ahead; Mason uses Clyde's suspected crime for personal and professional gain. And Mason views that gain *not* just as legal and political, but also social, as quoted above. Mason may despise the social status of the Griffiths family, but at the same time that status is the height to which he aspires. In other words, he is driven by envy.

Not only does Mason manipulate the judicial calendar, but he also withholds evidence from the defense, and, unknown to him, the evidence has been tampered with. Up to this point in the interrogation, Clyde has denied having a camera with him in the boat. But Mason has recovered the tripod and camera and believes the camera to be the murder weapon. (Dreiser's change from the tennis racquet of the actual case to a camera adds to the ambiguity of what happens on the boat. A camera on a boat at a scenic location is more plausible [Pizer "*American Tragedy*" 62].) Under the rules of evidence Mason must reveal the finding of the camera to the defense. He chooses instead to withhold the information. In an even more sinister turn of events, the withheld evidence has been tampered with, unknown to Mason, by his assistant, Burton Burleigh, who plants two of Roberta's hairs on the camera in order to seal the state's case. Burleigh "was convinced that Clyde had murdered the girl in cold blood. And for want of a bit of incriminating proof, was such a young, silent, vain crook as this to be allowed to escape?" (Dreiser 575). Burleigh has already made a decision of guilt that, in our system, is supposed to be left to a jury. That lack of a "bit of incriminating proof" is meant to protect the innocent from being found guilty. If that philosophy sometimes means that a guilty man goes free, that is the choice we have made as a society, not a choice to be tampered with by an individual. Mason's reaction to this incriminating evidence is to keep it from the opposition:

> . . . deciding for the present, at least, not to say anything in connection with the camera—to seal, if possible, the mouth of every one who knew. For, assuming that Clyde persisted in denying that he had carried a camera, or that his own lawyer should be unaware of the existence of such evidence, then how damning in court, and out of a clear sky, to produce this camera, these photographs of Roberta made by him, and the proof that the very measurements of one side of the camera coincided with the size of the wounds upon her face! How complete! How incriminating! (Dreiser 576)

How gleeful is Mr. Mason! His thoughts here remind us of the 1950s television character who always legally managed a surprise ending in court and who shares Mason's surname. In reality Mason has improperly withheld evidence from the defense.

The selection of defense counsel is not without its own political component. Samuel Griffiths, Clyde's uncle, knows that the family must provide an attorney to represent Clyde. Griffiths's personal attorney advises him that there are criminal lawyers in the larger cities of the state "deeply versed in the abstrusities and tricks of the criminal law" (Dreiser 588). These lawyers could probably save Clyde from the electric chair, but the process would expose the family to extensive publicity and to ridicule from an already incensed public. Griffiths chooses local counsel instead and thus deprives Clyde of the best representation that money could buy were Griffiths not so worried about his social standing. The local lawyer chosen is the political counterpart to the district attorney Mason. Alvin Belknap, a former state senator and assemblyman, is the Democrats' future hope for high office and a worthy courtroom opponent for the politically ambitious Republican Mason. In fact, Belknap is being considered for the same county judgeship nomination as Mason. Belknap acknowledges that the case cannot hurt him politically—at the very least he may be able to delay the proceedings until Mason is out of office and deprived of the publicity the trial will bring (Dreiser 591–93). "[Clyde's] guilt or innocence [becomes] less important than the outcome of the next local election" (Hayne 180). No one in the process is devoid of ulterior motives.

Once the attorneys are retained, Dreiser allows the reader to eavesdrop on several realistic defense strategy-planning sessions, where all of the options for defending Clyde are explored. One argument that could be made on behalf of Clyde would be that of insanity or "brain storm," but the Griffiths family will not permit such a defense, and, after all, they *are* paying the legal fees. Here Dreiser is emphasizing the influence that money can exert on the legal system, and the money is being used not in Clyde's best interest but to protect the Griffiths family. The lawyers determine that Roberta's letters are the most damaging part of the prosecution's case and that Clyde must testify in his own defense. Belknap's partner, Jephson, willing to consider any option in order to save Clyde, ultimately fashions the story Clyde tells on the stand. Though this may be viewed as merely aggressive lawyering, there is a difference between crafting a story and suborning perjury. Clyde himself is not entirely comfortable with Jephson's tactics, but he is willing to embrace the "change of heart" defense Jephson creates. As Strychacz notes, "Jephson . . . 'stories' in such a way as to undo the criminality of Clyde's plot" (103). "Storying" plays a major role in Dreiser's trial scene just as it does in any trial where each side constructs a version of events most favorable to its position.

Dreiser handles the grand jury proceeding in a single sentence, and then describes the pretrial motion of Belknap and Jephson for a change of venue, which is denied. Mason continues to investigate and to withhold what he has found from the defense.

Just as he chose to emphasize the backgrounds and planning sessions of the attorneys and to deemphasize the grand jury proceeding, Dreiser selects carefully when describing what goes on in the courtroom. The trial, covering 112 pages or approximately fourteen per cent of the narrative, begins in Chapter 19 of Book Three (Dreiser 629–741). Dreiser describes the circus-like atmosphere: " 'Peanuts!' 'Popcorn!' 'Hotdogs!' 'Get the story of Clyde Griffiths, with all the letters of Roberta Alden. Only twenty-five cents!' " (630). At this point the lawyers and the author are engaged in a very similar process. The district attorney and staff are arranging the order of evidence and directing or instructing the various witnesses, and the defense attorneys are coaching Clyde on his demeanor and his "change of heart" testimony to marry Roberta after all. The district attorney must tell a story that will persuade the jury that Clyde is guilty of murder. The defense attorney must tell a story that will convince the jury that

Clyde is not guilty. The author must tell a story in the courtroom that supports the major themes of the text. Dreiser too is deciding who will speak at the trial, what they will say, and in what order.

In an actual trial the next step is jury selection. A panel of jurors, drawn by the procedure mandated by the jurisdiction, is brought into the courtroom and questioned, either individually or as a group, by either the judge or the attorneys. Jurors are asked questions about their age; address; marital status; occupation; affiliations; and any physical or mental disabilities that would disqualify them from serving. They may be asked whether they or any member of their family has been the victim of a violent crime. They are usually introduced to the attorneys and the defendant and asked if they know any of the parties. They are read a list of potential witnesses and asked if they know any of them. Each side gets a number of challenges for cause to dismiss a particular juror, for example, if a potential juror demonstrates racial or religious prejudice, and a number of preemptory challenges that can be used for any reason, for example, if the attorney simply has a "bad feeling" about a particular juror. Nowadays in serious cases where the defendant can afford it, a jury consultant, often a psychologist, is brought in to advise the defense attorney on the selection of jurors who will be sympathetic to the defendant's case.

In *An American Tragedy* the courtroom and the jury selection are described through Clyde's eyes. Clyde's mind wanders as he tries to distract himself during the tedious process of picking a jury. As his eyes roam around the room, he uses physical landmarks such as "next to the wall," "five rows from them," and "this side of that third window from the front" to ground his thoughts. We hear Clyde's thoughts at this point because they are more interesting and more relevant to the narrative than the often boring process of jury selection. Dreiser tells us jury selection takes five days but, except for the first day in court, he sums up the experience in two sentences at the beginning of Chapter 20. He is assuring dramatic pace by eliminating a less important aspect of the trial to move quickly to Mason's opening statement.

Opening statements are to advise the jurors of the theory and main points of each side's case. In opening statements the lawyers introduce themselves and try to establish a rapport with the jurors. The attorneys are not supposed to argue their positions or present their personal opinions, but to give an overview of the evidence that their witnesses will be presenting. Naturally, each attorney presents the facts in the light most favorable to his case. Each may also choose to highlight the statutory elements of the offense for which the defendant is being tried. The defense usually has the choice of presenting its opening statement after the prosecution or of reserving that statement for presentation at the beginning of the defense case-in-chief. Belknap's opening is reserved until the defense case-in-chief begins later in the narrative.

The prosecutor's opening in *An American Tragedy* covers eight pages (Dreiser 639–47). "It was as if some one had suddenly exclaimed: 'Lights! Camera!' " (Dreiser 639). Mason asserts that his motive is to have justice done, a questionable assertion from the reader's perspective, knowing what the reader knows about the pretrial maneuvering. He reviews the facts of the case, emphasizing Roberta's humble background and Clyde's royal Griffiths blood. Dreiser has Mason employ all of the tactics taught to first-year law students: the finger pointing at the defendant for emphasis, the repetition of a key word ("the people *charge*"), a scornful smile when speaking about the defendant, and a reverential tone when mentioning the victim. Even the unsophisticated Clyde sees through the tactics being used, but his response can only be one of fear: "Clyde, terrorized by the force and the vehemence of it all, was chiefly concerned to note how much of exaggeration and unfairness was in all this" (Dreiser 644). Since Clyde has more information than the jury and knows the real story, he has good reason to worry that they will accept this exaggerated version of events. For his finale, Mason promises to produce an eyewitness: "Mason had no eye witness, but he could not resist this opportunity to throw so disrupting a thought into the opposition camp" (Dreiser 647). Belknap's response to the announcement of a surprise witness is to assure his client that Mason is bluffing, but Belknap also notes alternative approaches the defense can use if Mason is telling the truth, including buying time by cross-examining witnesses "by the week" in order to delay the trial until Mason is out of office.

It is unclear whether or not Dreiser knew that "surprise" witnesses are not permitted under the rules of most jurisdictions. Both sides must supply a list of witnesses in advance to the opposition. This rule is based on a principle of fairness in trial preparation. In Dreiser's scenario, it would be unfair to produce a witness for which defense counsel could not have prepared. The rule against surprise witnesses is also a way to avoid any conflicts of interest between the jurors and the witnesses. The list of witnesses is usually read to a prospective juror so he or she can state any potential conflict before being sworn.

Once Mason has completed his opening statement, he is ready to begin his case-in-chief. In the case-in-chief the prosecutor questions his witnesses on direct examination and the defense attorney questions those witnesses on cross-examination. On direct, the lawyer may not ask leading questions. On cross, the attorney may ask leading questions but only within the scope of the direct examination; he may not introduce any new topics. Once cross-examination is completed, the prosecutor has the opportunity to ask questions on redirect, but only within the scope of cross-examination; opposing counsel may then ask questions on recross, but again only within the scope of issues covered in redirect testimony. In theory, the examination of witnesses is a self-limiting endeavor.

To those readers who find Dreiser's prose long-winded, the first sentence of Chapter 21, introducing the prosecutor's case-in-chief, must be especially daunting: "And then witnesses, witnesses, witnesses—to the number of one hundred and twenty-seven" (648). We are told these include doctors, hiking guides, and the woman who heard

Roberta's last cry. But Dreiser carefully selects the witnesses whose testimony will be heard in part or in full. Titus Alden, Roberta's father, is called by the prosecution to elicit sympathy for the victim's family and used by Dreiser to illustrate this trial tactic and how the defense can counter with a series of objections to a witness of this type. Dreiser does not present the testimony word for word but alternates questions and answers with summarized portions of the testimony that details Roberta's move to Lycurgus. Finally Mason has Roberta's trunk brought into the courtroom and her possessions are paraded before the jury. Is this information relevant? The defense objects at the beginning of the testimony, but Mason promises to "connect it up." Relying on the district attorney's word, the judge allows the prosecution to proceed, but when Mason cannot "connect it up," the judge is forced to sustain the defense's objection and order the testimony stricken from the record. A useless foray on the part of the prosecution, you say? To the contrary. The jury has seen the victim's grief-stricken father and heard the victim's story whether or not that story remains a part of the official record. This is the infamous "unringing the bell" principle—once the bell is rung and the testimony has been heard, the damage has already been done, despite the repeated objections of the defense. The district attorney has scored points. But Belknap is not to be so easily outdone. He questions Mason's tactics, and Mason asks who is running the prosecution. Belknap replies, "The Republican candidate for county judge in this county, I believe!" The audience laughs, Mason accuses Belknap of trying to inject politics into the trial, and the judge reprimands both sides (Dreiser 649–50). It is Dreiser who has reminded us of the political motives of the characters.

Next the district attorney calls a series of witnesses to set the scene for Roberta's life in Lycurgus and her relationship with Clyde: Roberta's friend; Roberta's landlords; supervisors at the factory; Clyde's landlady; Roberta's mother; Clyde's society acquaintances; the druggist from whom Clyde sought information about an abortion; the doctor to whom he was referred; the neighbor of Roberta's parents whose telephone she used to contact Clyde; and the local mailman. Dreiser presents the testimony of these witnesses and those who saw Clyde and Roberta on their mountain trip in summary form. At the end of the tenth day of the trial, Belknap protests Mason's withholding of evidence as to the trip—guest registers with false names in Clyde's handwriting as verified by handwriting experts (Dreiser 651–55).

Dreiser's decision to use the summary technique for many of the witnesses could have been based on his judgment that the testimony of minor witnesses would not serve his thematic purposes and would dilute the dramatic quality of the trial, and he would certainly have been correct that listening to testimony from minor and expert witnesses is often tedious. But the decision may also have been more practical. Pizer points out that the 2,000 page Gillette transcript contained the testimony of many minor and expert witnesses that was merely summarized in the *New York World*, the main source of Dreiser's information (*"American Tragedy"* 57).

The eleventh day of the trial begins with Dreiser presenting summaries of the testimony of more witnesses to Clyde's actions before the crime. The existence of the camera is revealed, along with Clyde's reaction to that revelation. Over the next few days five doctors who examined Roberta's body testify as to their findings, and Mason puts Burleigh on the stand to perjure himself by testifying that he found Roberta's hairs on the camera. The woman who heard Roberta's last cry also testifies (Dreiser 655–60). Mason's final evidence, the love letters of Roberta to Clyde, is carefully calculated to elicit the greatest emotional response from the jury at the end of the prosecutor's case. As he reads the letters into the record, he cries, and as he rests his case, Roberta's mother faints.

Dreiser is at his best here in creating an effective trial scene. In the Gillette trial the letters of Grace Brown were read into the record by the district attorney as they occurred in the chronology of events, that is, *before* the testimony concerning the final trip and the medical testimony. There could have been many reasons for this sequence, including the unavailability of the doctors or a miscalculation on the part of the district attorney or merely the desire for a chronological structure to the case, but surely the most effective use of the victim's "voice," or her story in her own words, is as a climax to the prosecution's case. Dreiser used the letters in *An American Tragedy* for dramatic effect, and some of the letters are in whole or in part the letters actually written by Grace Brown. Pizer tells us that Dreiser used some letters in the body of the narrative—at the time Roberta wrote them and Clyde received them—and has Mason read only six carefully chosen passages at trial for the greatest emotional impact. "Dreiser mixed verbatim quotations, loose paraphrase, and new material—yet maintained the emotional texture of alternating pleading and recrimination, and hope and fear, of the original letters" (Pizer "*American Tragedy*" 66–67).

Defense counsel, having reserved his opening statement, is now ready to open and present his case-in-chief. The procedure for the defense case will be the same as for the prosecution except that the roles of the attorneys will be reversed: the defense counsel will examine on direct and the district attorney will cross-examine the witnesses.

Belknap faces a hostile audience as he makes his opening statement. The jury and the audience have heard three weeks of prosecution evidence. Belknap emphasizes that only the defense knows the truth and cautions the jury not to be swayed by circumstantial evidence. He makes a passing remark on the "politically biased prosecution" and asks that the male jurors remember "we were once all boys." He admits that Clyde loves "Miss X," as the parties have agreed to call Sondra in order to protect her reputation, but states that Clyde and Roberta were never formally engaged. Instead Clyde offered Roberta the opportunity to be supported but to live apart; she insisted on marriage. Now what was he supposed to do? Belknap labels Clyde a mental and moral coward. He is afraid of the social mistake and the sin of pursuing the relationship with Roberta, and he fears the consequences of his behavior. Finally, it is mental and moral cowardice that makes Clyde conceal Roberta's death. Belknap ends his statement by indicating that the person from whom the jurors need to hear the story is Clyde.

Dreiser does the best he can in crafting an opening when Belknap is denied the use of the strongest argument in favor of Clyde's actions, that of diminished capacity or insanity. Belknap is right to admit some of the prosecution's contentions but vehemently to deny that Clyde intended to kill Roberta. The "mental and moral fear complex" argument seems risky since the jury can decide that cowardice is no excuse for crime, as Belknap admits, but here the writer rather than the lawyer takes over the speech. Dreiser needs to reinforce the idea that society's rules have a negative effect on the less privileged. Through Belknap Dreiser can emphasize that, after getting a co-worker pregnant, Clyde has good reason to be afraid of the social system to which he aspires. Clyde can imagine what his wealthy relatives will think of his conduct. He will be ostracized. He will certainly lose the woman he loves along with her lifestyle. And he will bring shame on his parents. Dreiser wants to highlight the fact that these are dire consequences for having sex.

In a change of plans, Jephson rather than Belknap conducts the direct examination of Clyde (Dreiser 673–702). Clyde begins with his birth, his life as a bellboy in Kansas City, his two years of wandering after he and some friends are in a car that strikes and kills a child, and his work in Chicago, where he meets his uncle who offers him a job. Just as he did for Roberta's father, Dreiser chooses a question-and-answer format for the beginning of Clyde's testimony. Mason objects repeatedly and his objections are usually sustained by the judge. Through frequent objections early in the direct examination that interrupt the flow of testimony, Mason is attempting to fluster either the examiner or the witness.

Dreiser alternates between summarizing Clyde's testimony and presenting it in question-and-answer format. This method serves several purposes. It allows Dreiser to move quickly through parts of Clyde's life with which the reader is already familiar and to dramatize the sections of testimony that support the "mental and moral cowardice" theory of the defense and support Dreiser's themes. For example, the events of Clyde's life after his arrival in Lycurgus are summarized, but the question-and-answer format is used on the issue of Clyde's feelings for Roberta and Sondra. In addition Dreiser interjects the conflicts between the attorneys during the question-and-answer portions of the text. At one point Mason and Jephson argue over whose witnesses are being led like parrots. A scuffle is about to break out and the attorneys must be restrained by court personnel.

Clyde begins to tell the story, created for him by Jephson in Belknap's office, about what happened on the lake. This is also a story created by Dreiser; no information about what happened in the boat appeared in the evidence presented at trial in the Gillette case (Lingeman, *Journey* 245). By including this information, Dreiser illustrates the ambivalence of someone trapped by personal desires and social forces. Clyde says he still had no plan as to Roberta, and *she* suggested the trip to the Adirondacks. She said she just wanted to get married to give the baby a name and then she would go away. Clyde testifies that he had a change of heart and decided that he would marry Roberta, but he did not tell her yet. He was going to tell her that day on the lake. Then he describes the accident:

> "I called to her to try to get to the boat—it was moving away—to take hold of it, but she didn't seem to hear me or understand what I meant. I was afraid to go too near her at first because she was striking out in every direction—and before I could swim ten strokes forward her head had gone down once and come up and then gone down again for a second time. By then the boat had floated all of thirty or forty feet away and I knew that I couldn't get her into that. And then I decided that if I wanted to save myself I had better swim ashore." (Dreiser 700)

Jephson has coached his client well. The story blends fact and half-truths in a way that makes it plausible to the jury and psychologically satisfying to Clyde by resolving his personal doubts. This version of events is really a retelling of the little voice in Clyde's head that counseled him to save himself. He did save himself that day on the lake, and he hopes to do so again on the witness stand. When questioned by Jephson, after affirming that he understands what it means to tell the whole truth, Clyde denies striking Roberta in the boat, throwing her into the lake, willfully upsetting the boat, or causing her death. Then comes the last question on direct examination:

> "You swear that it was an accident—unpremeditated and undesigned by you?"
> "I do," lied Clyde, who felt that in fighting for his life he was telling a part of the truth, for that accident was unpremeditated and undesigned. It had not been as he had planned and he could swear to that. (Dreiser 701–2)

Mason's cross-examination of Clyde fills the next thirty-one pages of text (Dreiser 702–33). Dreiser uses a question-and-answer format for this testimony as Mason jumps from topic to topic in an attempt to unnerve Clyde (Pizer "*American Tragedy*" 65). Both Lingeman and Pizer note that Dreiser writes a more effective cross-examination for Mason than the prosecutor at the Gillette trial actually performed (*Journey* 251; "*American Tragedy*" 66). The result is a devastating attack on Clyde, substantively and psychologically. Obviously Mason focuses on the weaknesses in the defense case such as registering in three different hotels under three different names, the expectation of marriage in Roberta's letters, and the fact that Clyde originally lied about not having a camera with him. Belknap objects frequently during the cross-examination. At one point he is successful, and Mason's thoughts sum up the tactic being used: " 'Well, to go on,' proceeded Mason, now more nettled and annoyed than ever by this watchful effort on the part of Belknap and Jephson to break the force and significance of his each and every attack, and all the more determined not to be outdone . . . " (Dreiser 717). But if anyone can be annoying it is Mason with his sneers and his sarcastic tone of voice. He frequently manages to rephrase Clyde's answers or to denigrate what Clyde has said. He often makes speeches in the guise of asking a question, to which Belknap properly objects:

> "Remember her writing you this?" And here Mason picked up and opened one of the letters and began reading. . . . "Does that seem at all sad to you?"
> "Yes, sir, it does."
> "Did it then?"
> "Yes, sir, it did."
> "You knew it was sincere, didn't you?" snarled Mason.
> "Yes, sir. I did."
> "Then why didn't a little of that pity that you claim moved you so deeply out there in the center of Big Bittern move you down there in Lycurgus to pick up the telephone there in Mrs. Peyton's house where you were and reassure that lonely girl by so much as a word that you were coming? Was it because your pity for her then wasn't as great as it was after she wrote you that threatening letter? Or was it because you had a plot and you were afraid that too much telephoning to her might attract attention? How was it that you had so much pity all of a sudden up at Big Bittern, but none at all down there at Lycurgus? Is it something you can turn on and off like a faucet?" (Dreiser 704)

Dreiser stage-manages the cross-examination very effectively. Early in the cross, Mason has the rowboat brought into the courtroom, hands Clyde the camera, and asks him to demonstrate exactly what happened on the lake. (This reenactment never occurred at the Gillette trial.) Belknap objects but after argument his objection is overruled. Someone plays the role of Roberta, and Mason tells Clyde to "direct" her actions. Belknap continues to object on the basis that the demonstration cannot possibly be conducted under the same circumstances in a courtroom as on a lake. Mason asks, " 'Then you refuse to allow this demonstration to be made?' " (Dreiser 706). Mason has forced Belknap into a corner, and Belknap now has a tough decision to make. If he refuses to permit the demonstration to go forward, it will seem as though his client has something to hide. If he allows Mason to proceed, Belknap has no way of knowing or controlling what will happen. Belknap feigns indifference: " 'Oh, make it if you choose. It doesn't mean anything though, as anybody can see,' persisted Belknap, suggestively" (Dreiser 706). The impression left at the end of the demonstration is that, based on the evidence of injuries to Roberta, Clyde must have hit her harder than he did in court. Mason's second bit of showmanship occurs when he hands Clyde a lock of Roberta's hair "more to torture Clyde than anything else—to wear him down nervously. . . . " Clyde recoils. " 'Oh, don't be afraid,' persisted Mason, sardonically. 'It's only your dead love's hair' " (Dreiser 713).

But Mason's strength is his ability to catch Clyde in lies, especially concerning whether or not Clyde had a plan in mind all along. Mason asks Clyde to account for the twenty dollars Clyde claims to have spent on the trip. Clyde cannot account for every cent, and Mason points out that Clyde has forgotten the cost of the boat rental at Big Bittern. Instead of relying on the answer "I didn't notice" that he uses elsewhere in his testimony, Clyde makes up an answer and is trapped. Mason is able to show not only that Clyde does not know the cost of the boat because he never asked—since he never expected to return—but also that he has just lied about it on the stand. For his last line of questions, Mason is equally effective in demonstrating that Clyde lied when he said he got the maps and brochures about the Adirondacks at the hotel in Utica. Mason passes the brochures, stamped with the name of a hotel in Lycurgus, to the jurors. Once again this evidence is doubly damaging—a lie and proof of premeditation. Mason knows a powerful conclusion when he sees one, and he ends his cross-examination.

Dreiser summarizes the testimony of the eleven remaining witnesses, seven for Clyde and four for Mason. Mason's witnesses

are presumably called as rebuttal witnesses after the defense has
rested.   Dreiser does not go into this procedural detail but does
indicate that the prosecution witnesses contradict defense testimony,
the purpose of rebuttal witnesses.

Closing arguments are just that, arguments that summarize the
testimony and present the conclusions to be reached based on that
testimony. Unlike opening statements, an attorney here may give his
own opinion and characterize the evidence to fit his theory of the case.
The attorney points out subtleties and connections that may not have
been apparent to the jurors. The jurors decide the facts of the case,
but the lawyer's job in closing argument is to help the jurors see *his*
version of the facts.

Dreiser presents the closing arguments in summary form, a choice
that seems odd at first because in many cases these speeches provide
some of the most dramatic moments of the trial. When considering
Dreiser's purpose, however, one sees that Clyde's reactions have been
the focus of the trial scene, and Clyde is already exhausted by the
process culminating in his intensive cross-examination. To Clyde the
closings are merely to be endured. And it takes endurance because we
are told that each side speaks for an entire day. Belknap closes first,
retracing much of his opening statement. Pizer tells us that since
Dreiser took material from the defense attorney's closing argument at
the Gillette trial and used it in Belknap's opening statement, the reader
has already heard that information ("*American Tragedy*" 65). Belknap
reiterates his theme of mental and moral cowardice and warns the
jurors not to allow their sympathy for the victim to sway them to
convict Clyde for a crime of which he is not guilty. He goes on to
cite again the circumstantial nature of the evidence and repeat that
only Clyde knows what happened, and Clyde has clearly explained the
events. Belknap explains away such evidence as the brochures, the
price of the boat, the burying of the tripod as either "accidents of
chance, or memory," and Clyde's failure to rescue Roberta as a result
of Clyde's confusion—" 'hesitating fatally but not criminally.' "

Mason's closing argument for the prosecution focuses on Clyde's lies, reiterates the testimony of the witnesses, and plays on the jurors' sympathy for the victim. After hearing Mason, Clyde decides "no jury such as this was likely to acquit him in the face of evidence so artfully and movingly recapitulated" (Dreiser 734–35).

Just as the jurors are responsible for determining the facts of the case, the judge is responsible for providing the law that the jurors are to apply to those facts when deliberating. In his instructions the judge normally reads the applicable criminal statute to the jury and reviews the elements of the crime. He reminds the jurors that the burden of proof is on the prosecution and that they must be convinced "beyond a reasonable doubt" that the defendant is guilty in order to convict. The judge, of course, covers any other point of law that may be relevant in the case. The judge in *An American Tragedy* instructs the jury that circumstantial evidence is often more reliable than direct evidence, that proof of motive is not necessary for conviction, and that the defendant had no duty of rescue toward the drowning Roberta. Only if the defendant intentionally brought about or contributed to the accident can he be found guilty (Dreiser 735–36).[4] These instructions are reasonable if a bit brief considering a man's life is at stake, although Dreiser's version is almost identical to the charge in the Gillette trial (Fishkin 119).

The judge and the lawyers retire to a nearby hotel for dinner and drinks as the jury deliberates. In Dreiser's world we are privy to information about the deliberations that would never be found in a transcript. We are told that one man, politically opposed to Mason and sympathetic to Belknap and Jephson, holds out for five ballots. He is then persuaded, however, that it would be in his own best economic interest as the owner of a local drugstore not to be discovered as the one responsible for a hung jury, and he goes along with the majority. Belknap believes in the theory that a jury that won't look you in the eye when it reenters the courtroom after deliberations is one that is about to convict your client, and no one looks at

Belknap, Jephson, or Clyde as the jurors return. The verdict is guilty
of murder in the first degree. Clyde asks that a telegram be sent to
his mother. Later, as he listens from his cell, the crowds cheer for
Mason.

The Griffiths family refuses to fund Clyde's appeal, and Belknap
and Jephson are also unwilling to bear the cost of what they see as an
expensive undertaking (Dreiser 745–46). In order to fund her trip east
for the sentencing, Clyde's mother hires herself out as a reporter for
a Denver paper. While in New York, she is encouraged by Belknap
and Jephson to give speeches in defense of her son in order to raise
money for his appeal. She manages to raise about half the money
necessary before her husband becomes ill and she must return to
Denver. Ironically, it is a fellow inmate at Auburn penitentiary,
Nicholson, a lawyer convicted of poisoning a wealthy elderly client,
who advises Clyde on the best argument for his appeal:

> [T]hat the admission of Roberta's letters as evidence, as they stood, at least,
> be desperately fought on the ground that the emotional force of them was
> detrimental in the case of any jury anywhere, to a calm unbiased consider-
> ation of the material facts presented by them—and that instead of the letters
> being admitted as they stood they should be digested for the facts alone and
> that digest—and that only offered to the jury. (Dreiser 775)

Clyde's attorneys agree to pursue the appeal, including this argument,
but to no avail. The Court of Appeals affirms the decision of the
lower court. The appellate court notes the circumstantial nature of the
evidence, " 'But taken all together and considered as a connected
whole, [the facts] make such convincing proof of guilt . . . ' " (Dreiser
799). Clyde has one last hope: a commutation of his sentence from
death to life in prison by the governor. His mother arrives to plead
personally for her son's life, and she is accompanied by the Rev.
Duncan McMillan, to whom Clyde has confessed his true, confused
feelings about what occurred on the lake. When the governor asks
McMillan if he knows of any "material fact" that would invalidate or

weaken the testimony presented at trial, McMillan responds, " 'As his spiritual advisor I have entered only upon the spiritual, not the legal aspect of his life' " (Dreiser 803). McMillan does not take advantage of this final opportunity to describe Clyde's obsession with Sondra, which was withheld from consideration at trial. The governor rejects this appeal as well as another by telegram just two days before Clyde's execution in the electric chair.

Was Clyde Griffiths guilty of murder in the first degree? This question was the topic of a national essay contest sponsored by Dreiser's publishers Boni and Liveright in 1926. Appropriately, a lawyer supplied the best answer. Law professor Albert H. Lévitt of Washington and Lee University won the five hundred dollar prize. His essay, formally published for the first time in a 1991 article by Philip Gerber, presents an excellent overview of the law of the case as well as addressing the many social issues involved. To Lévitt there is no single answer to the question of guilt but a series of answers based on the perspective from which one views the events: "1. The answer given by the law governing murder in the first degree. 2. An answer based upon a system of Christian ethics. 3. An answer based upon the facts as the jury saw them. 4. An answer based upon the societal conditions under which Clyde Griffiths lived" (qtd. in Gerber 222). It is easy to understand why Lévitt won the contest. He crafted a response that would satisfy every reader of the novel.

As for guilt as it accrues outside of the courtroom, Lévitt finds Clyde guilty under Christian ethics. "I can see no excuse for Clyde in morals" (qtd. in Gerber 231). Society also bears some responsibility for its failure to adequately address issues of sex education, birth control and abortion, and capital punishment. While Lévitt agrees that Clyde should be executed, he declares that the state shares blame for the social conditions that produced Clyde (Gerber 241).

Lévitt understands completely why the jury found Clyde guilty, based on the facts as they were presented by the attorneys and the law as it was presented by the judge. The jury did not believe that the capsizing was an accident or that Clyde had changed his mind and therefore had no intent to commit a crime, and their beliefs were reasonable. Under these circumstances, the jury had no choice but to convict Clyde. For Lévitt moral guilt can be imputed to Clyde for his failure to save Roberta, to society for its failure to properly raise Clyde, but not to the jurors for their reasonable conclusions.

Lévitt's answer to the question of legal guilt is one of the clearest presentations of the law as it applies to this case. A crime consists of an act or omission that is the proximate cause of the injury and the concurrent intent to commit that act or omission. Clyde may have planned a murder, but, based on his thoughts at the time of the capsizing, he lacked the requisite intent to commit the crime at the time of the act. In other words, the capsizing was an accident that caused Roberta's death (Gerber 228). As to the omission of not saving Roberta from drowning, Lévitt points out that without a legal duty of rescue, of which none exists under these facts, there can be no legally culpable omission (Gerber 229). Clyde had no duty to rescue Roberta and therefore cannot be held legally responsible for her death. The correct answer to the question of whether Clyde was legally guilty of murder in the first degree is no.

Based on Dreiser's purpose of examining societal issues both in and beyond the courtroom, it would be unfair to demand any more than a reasonable representation of what happens during a trial. Dreiser gives a reasonable representation; he effectively describes both the strengths and the weaknesses of our legal system. Mona G. Rosenman in her article on *An American Tragedy* holds Dreiser to a constitutional standard within which to make his thematic point. She is correct that the conduct of the district attorney at Clyde's trial, including his prejudicial statements and his efforts to hold the trial as quickly as possible, would constitute reversible error on appeal. But the most Dreiser can be accused of here is exaggerating what goes on to a certain degree in at least some of the trials held every day in this country. Yes, Dreiser illustrated violations of due process under the

Fourteenth Amendment—that was his point, not something for which he should be condemned.

Rosenman admits that Dreiser deliberately introduced material not present in the accounts of the actual case:

> Of course, Dreiser deliberately introduced this material for the purpose of showing just how unfairly Clyde was treated. Any attorney could have told Dreiser then, as he would now, that Mason's remarks not only disqualified him as prosecuting attorney but also guaranteed—should he insist on prosecuting the case—that the next highest court would reverse any decision made by the trial court adverse to the accused. (14)

Yet Rosenman in her argument seems to demand that Dreiser should have presented a case without constitutional error. She cites the case of Sam Sheppard, where a 1954 conviction was overturned when an appeals court ruled that the trial court had improperly denied a change of venue in a situation where the community had been inflamed by the extensive press coverage of the case, as Clyde's attorneys also alleged in their denied motion for a change of venue. Rosenman credits a young F. Lee Bailey with winning the reversal and Sheppard's later acquittal in the death of his wife. We should all be so lucky to be able to afford F. Lee Bailey as our attorney; Bailey costs money. Sheppard was an affluent neurosurgeon who had access to his own source of funds, unlike Clyde, whose uncle provided the funds but acted in his own best interest, not in Clyde's best interest. Rosenman states that if Clyde's attorneys had used a Fourteenth Amendment due process argument and claimed that Clyde had not received a fair trial, as was argued in the Sheppard case, then Clyde's conviction would have been overturned. Rosenman is probably right, but that result would not have served Dreiser's larger purpose of bringing to the reader's attention the issue of whether society was placing unreasonable burdens on individuals in pursuit of the American Dream.

Sally Day Trigg is more in tune with Dreiser's purpose. She concludes her article on the criminal justice system in *An American*

Tragedy with the following summary:

> The trial he describes is a travesty. The men who direct the proceedings are adversaries focused more on victory and political prizes than on truth. The jury, primed by sensational press accounts, is the epitome of partiality, basing their judgments on biases, emotions, and public opinion. And the defendant is a mechanism, constructed by the forces of society and by his own nature, and lacking the free will assumed by the law. He cowers in the face of the crowd that craves his death because they despise his immorality and his association with wealth. And finally, Dreiser damns the cruelty and inhumanity of Death Row, the condemned man's last stop before society slaughters him. (438)

Trigg is right: "The goal of the ideal trial is to accurately determine the facts of an event so that a fact finder can decide if the actions of an individual fulfill the requirements of a statute" (430). This would be an *ideal* trial. Instead, in Dreiser's account and in our courts, we have an adversarial system where winning counts, where shading the facts is the lawyers' job, and where the "performance ability" of the lawyers counts more than the facts (Trigg 430–432).

Our system is not perfect, but even Dreiser, who spent much of his life questioning the system, could not offer a better alternative. The fact that critics like Rosenman and Trigg, and a lawyer like Lévitt, take Dreiser's depiction so seriously is itself testimony to the effectiveness of his trial scenes.

Why does Dreiser give us the trial in such detail? Certainly he is criticizing the criminal justice system in which Clyde is enmeshed. Hayne believes "what is restored at the end of *An American Tragedy* looks much more like the continuation of chaos" (182). McWilliams notes that as Dreiser was writing *An American Tragedy*, Roscoe Pound, the legal scholar and writer, was lecturing against the flaws in American criminal procedure, such as prejudiced jurors, ambitious prosecutors, the tendency of the media to turn a trial into a circus, and monetary motivation in a trial, all of which occur in Dreiser's narrative (93). Both *An American Tragedy* and *Native Son* show "politically ambitious district attorneys, inept lawyers, an aggressive press, and hostile public opinion as features of the American criminal justice system of the time. In [neither case] is there a change of venue or effective control of the press" (Friedland xxii). Dreiser mirrors the concerns of his time, but he goes beyond the flaws in the system to highlight the flaws in society as a whole—a society that tempts everyone equally with the American Dream of wealth, success, and social acceptance at the same time that it denies a large segment of the population the means, through education and employment, to attain that dream.

NOTES

1. The articles were originally commissioned and published in the *New York Post* in 1934 and in an expanded version in *Mystery Magazine* in 1935. References are to a reprint of the articles with an introduction by Jack Saltzman in 1972. In the articles Dreiser reported on the case of Robert Allen Edwards of Wilkes-Barre, Pennsylvania, who was convicted in 1934 of killing the pregnant Freda McKechnie in order to marry Margaret Crain. Dreiser became interested in this case because of its striking similarity to the story he had told in *An American Tragedy*.

2. Hayne notes the interest in the Gillette case continues unabated.

> Two examinations of the facts surrounding the Gillette case have been published in the last few years: Joseph W. Brownell and Patricia A. Wawrzaszek *Adirondack Tragedy: The Gillette Murder Case of 1906* (Interlaken, NY: Heart of the Lakes Publishing[,] 1986), and Craig Brandon *Murder in the Adirondacks: An American Tragedy Revisited* (Utica: North Country Books[,] 1986). (185 note 9)

3. Castle worked with the transcript itself and a microfilm copy of the abstract of the facts of the case contained in the Court of Appeals opinion along with newspaper accounts (iii). The conclusions he reached:

> 1. The characters, situations, and incidents, together with a wealth of supporting details are drawn from the documents of the Gillette case; furthermore, the total structure of time, place[,] and action of the Gillette

case is maintained in *An American Tragedy*, Dreiser supplying for the total structure only the portion devoted to the youth of Clyde Griffiths, i.e., the first 147 pages of the novel.

2. Approximately 190 pages of *An American Tragedy* closely parallel the original materials both in the outline of incidents and the supporting details.

3. In the process of adapting the materials of the Gillette case to the novel, Dreiser either carelessly or purposely transferred to *An American Tragedy* about two thousand words verbatim. With the exception of Roberta's letters, which came either from the court records or other newspapers, Dreiser apparently leaned most heavily upon the text of the New York *World* for material which could be used unchanged.

4. Approximately 220 pages of *An American Tragedy* appear to be direct extensions or expansions of facts or allegations which appear in the documents.

5. About fourteen pages of descriptive details of *An American Tragedy* seem to be the product of Dreiser's first-hand observation of the locality in which the principal action of the Gillette case occurred.

6. Compilation of total indebtedness shows that approximately one-half of *An American Tragedy* has solid basis in the materials of the Gillette case . . . (83–84). [citations to the 1947 World Publishing edition of *An American Tragedy*]

4. Friedland states "the facts would probably not have brought about a conviction for homicide at the time, but would probably do so today" and goes on to cite as an example a proposed section of the Canadian Criminal Code imposing a duty to rescue (xxix note 39).

II

Richard Wright's *Native Son*

Native Son, published in 1940, was the first work by an African-American writer to make the best-seller list (Reilly 35). Richard Wright read and was influenced by *An American Tragedy*, and his text echoes the themes of Dreiser's narrative. Wright's protagonist is not only a social and economic outsider but also an outsider by race. But, as McWilliams notes, while Clyde's crime increases his self-doubt, Bigger Thomas's crime gives him an identity (100). To that extent, Wright's character illustrates the beginning of a trend in these narratives toward criminals who rebel against a system ill-equipped to deal with those who live outside the law.

Wright wrote a twenty-five page description of the genesis of *Native Son* entitled "How 'Bigger' Was Born" in which he indicates the sources of the narrative. Wright's main character, Bigger Thomas, was a composite of five types of African-Americans identified by Wright, beginning with the local bully in Wright's hometown of Jackson, Mississippi (Wright, "Bigger" 22). Once Wright left the South, got in touch with his own feelings, and came in contact with the labor movement, he began to see Bigger as a symbol: "I made the discovery that Bigger Thomas was not black all the time; he was white, too, and there were literally millions of him, everywhere" (Wright, "Bigger" 28).

"How 'Bigger' Was Born" is a remarkable document not only

because it lists the sources of *Native Son* but also because it tells us of Wright's concerns about the response to his work by both blacks and whites. In the end, Wright wrote the narrative he had to write, regardless of people's reaction. Wright does an excellent job of explaining the technical aspects of the narrative. He says the plot of *Native Son* is "what had made [Bigger] and what he meant" and the one criterion of the narrative is "to tell the truth as I saw it and felt it" (Wright, "Bigger" 40, 43). Wright explains that he was trying to capture "the objective and subjective aspects of Bigger's life" by combining stream of consciousness, interior monologue, "direct rendering of a dream state," and "matter-of-fact depiction" (Wright, "Bigger" 43–44). Wright believes that "the main burden of all serious fiction consists almost wholly of character-destiny and the items, social, political, and personal, of that character-destiny" (Wright, "Bigger" 44). To convey that character destiny, Wright presents Bigger's story from Bigger's point of view in the present using long scenes against a unified background (Wright, "Bigger" 44–45).

Native Son is divided into three books: Fear, Flight, and Fate. Bigger Thomas's story is that of a twenty-year-old black man with an eighth-grade education who is unemployed and living in the slums of Chicago in a one-room apartment with his mother, younger brother, and sister. In Book One, "Fear," we meet Bigger on the day he begins a new job as a chauffeur for the wealthy, white Daltons. Bigger, given a room of his own and a good meal, is shown how to care for the furnace, one of his duties. He learns from Peggy, the housekeeper, that the Daltons' twenty-three-year-old daughter, Mary, has been hanging around with Communists, much to her parents' consternation. Bigger's first assignment is to drive Mary to a university class that evening. Mary has other plans: she has Bigger pick up her friend Jan Erlone at the Labor Defenders office and then asks Bigger to recommend a place to eat on the South Side, the black section of town. The trio eat together at Ernie's Kitchen Shack and drink afterwards in the car. As Bigger drives around the park, the couple make love in the back seat. Bigger drops Jan off after taking some Communist pamphlets from him and drives back to the Daltons' house with the drunk Mary. He manages to carry Mary up to her room and place her on her bed when her blind mother enters the room and speaks to Mary. Bigger is so afraid of being discovered in the bedroom of a drunken white woman at two in the morning that he puts a pillow over Mary's face to keep her quiet, and she suffocates. Bigger stuffs the body into the furnace only to discover that the furnace is not large enough for the entire body. Bigger uses first a knife and then a hatchet to decapitate the body and burns the evidence in the furnace.

In Book Two of the narrative, "Flight," Mary's absence is discovered, and Bigger, while visiting his girlfriend, Bessie Mears, gets the idea to send a ransom note when Bessie points out that the Daltons live in the same area as the Loeb family, whose son was involved in the Leopold-Loeb murder case where two teenaged university graduates kidnapped and killed a fourteen-year-old boy in their attempt to commit the "perfect crime." [1] Bigger signs the ransom note "Red" to cast further suspicion on Mary's friend, Jan, and the Communists.[2] The Daltons hold a news conference in their basement after which the reporters linger hoping for more information. Peggy reminds Bigger to clean the ashes out of the furnace and build a new fire. Since Bigger has good reason not to remove the ashes with the reporters watching, he adds more coal to the fire instead and causes thick smoke to fill the basement. A reporter offers to help, takes the shovel from Bigger's hands, scoops out the ashes, and reveals pieces of white bone among the ashes. Bigger sneaks out of the basement, goes to Bessie's, and together they run to an abandoned building to hide. By now Bessie has guessed that Bigger killed Mary. He cannot leave Bessie behind and he cannot escape with her along. After raping her, Bigger smashes Bessie's head in with a brick and drops her body down an air shaft. Eventually, after a building-by-building search of the Black Belt by the police, Bigger is trapped on the roof of a building and fire hoses are used to disarm him so he can be captured.

Book Three of the text, "Fate," follows Bigger's progress through the judicial system during which he pleads guilty to the murders of Mary and Bessie and is sentenced to death.

Wright said he wrote the first draft of *Native Son* in four months, and, when he was halfway through, the Robert Nixon case hit the Chicago papers (Wright, "Bigger" 43). Wright, living in New York, contacted his friend Margaret Walker in Chicago and asked her to send him the clippings on the case. For the next year Walker gathered information from five Chicago papers, including the *Tribune*, and eventually Wright had enough material to cover the floor of his nine-by-twelve bedroom in New York (M. Walker 122–23). "Many of the newspaper items and some of the incidents in *Native Son* are but fictionalized versions of the Robert Nixon case and rewrites of news stories from the *Chicago Tribune*" (Wright, "Bigger" 41). The critics disagree on exactly how much of Wright's narrative is based on press accounts ("major portions" M. Walker 123; "a few minor details" Fabre 172), but there are similarities between the facts of the Nixon case and Bigger's situation. Those similarities reflect Wright's point that there are many Biggers from the same environment caught in the same system. Wright does not give the facts of the Nixon case in "How 'Bigger' Was Born" but describes a "stereotyped situation" of the police picking up the first "unattached and homeless" young black man they find and holding him until he confesses:

> Why does he confess? After the boy has been grilled day and night, hanged up by his thumbs, dangled by his feet out of twenty-story windows, and beaten (in places that leave no scars—cops have found a way to do that), he signs the papers before him, papers which are usually accompanied by a verbal promise to the boy that he will not go to the electric chair. Of course, he ends up by being executed or sentenced for life. If you think I'm telling tall tales, get chummy with some white cop who works in a Black Belt district and ask him for the lowdown. (Wright, "Bigger" 41)

Fabre has provided some of the details of the Nixon case:

> On May 27, 1938, this eighteen-year-old black boy had taken a brick and murdered a woman, the mother of two, apparently because she surprised him in the act of robbing her apartment. He was immediately identified by his fingerprints and caught with bloodstains on his clothes while still in the vicinity of the crime, at which time he denounced an accomplice, a boy his own age named Earl Hicks. The Chicago police subsequently got him to confess, probably under torture, to another crime, two attacks also on white women as well as five attempted murders of which it was not at all certain he was guilty.
>
> . . . The *Tribune* had immediately transformed the murder into a sexual crime and made a great deal out of the charge of rape, although the prosecution never explicitly brought this charge against Nixon. . . .
>
> In addition to the black defense lawyers already on the case, the International Labor Defense appointed a white lawyer, Joseph Roth, to defend the accused. (Fabre 172)

The Nixon case pretrial was "a complicated series of confessions and repudiations, charges of police brutality, and dramatic outbursts of violence . . . " (Kinnamon, "Background" 70). Nixon's trial lasted one week, jury deliberations lasted one hour, and Nixon was sentenced to death (C. Blake 196). Fabre says Wright's interest in the Nixon case was "more out of a desire to study the behavior of Whites once they turned against a black man than out of curiosity about the psychology and motivation of the murderer himself " (172). Walker concurs: "Like Dreiser, Wright used newspaper clippings to help in the delineation of character. Truman Capote has done the same thing with *In Cold Blood* . . . " (M. Walker 125).

Besides making use of the newspaper accounts, Wright also did research on the scene in Chicago, as Dreiser had done in upstate New York.[3] Wright visited Ulysses S. Keys, the first black lawyer hired for Nixon, and obtained a copy of the brief Keys had written for the case before he was replaced by an N.A.A.C.P. lawyer. Wright went to the Cook County Jail, where Nixon was held. Walker tells how she took Wright to the library for books on the Leopold-Loeb trial and on Clarence Darrow, the defense attorney in the case (M. Walker 124–25). Wright used real-life models for the lawyers in *Native Son*. For State's Attorney Buckley the model was Attorney General Thomas Courtney, whom Wright had helped get elected; for Bigger's attorney, Boris Max, the model was an unnamed International Labor Defense official, whom Wright knew in Chicago during 1934. Max's defense of Bigger is based on Clarence Darrow's performance in the Leopold-Loeb case (Fabre 172–73).

One of the most controversial aspects of Wright's narrative is his use of Communist theories in Bigger's defense. The critics disagree on the extent and the effect of Communist doctrine in the text. Walker sees *Native Son* as "affected by a crude Marxism" and "consciously an effort to apply solutions to the problem of race with Communist ideology" (231–32). Bone says Wright "has failed to digest Communism artistically. . . . The Communist party is simply not strong enough as a symbol of relatedness. . . . He simply cannot fit the ideas of Bigger into those of the Communist party" (150–51). Kinnamon concurs:

> The courtroom arguments of Max in the final section, of course, are patently leftist. He equates racial and class prejudice, both being based on economic exploitation. . . . Not all of Max's courtroom speech reflects so directly communist doctrine, but none of it is inconsistent with the party line on racial matters. ("Background" 71)

On the other hand, Reilly points out:

> . . . in the 1930s and 1940s the Communist Party was exceptional enough in its support for Negro rights that the appearance of sympathy toward party figures in a novel written by a politically active black author in 1940 may be no more unusual than, say, the occurrence of New Deal sentiments in other fiction. (56–57)

For purposes of our discussion, Redden's observation is useful:

> For the sake of argument one can concede that Max's speech is
> forthrightly partisan, partly in the sense that it represents a lawyer defending
> his client in court, partly in that it serves as a vehicle for Wright's deeply
> felt ideas about racism, but it is not primarily, or even significantly, a
> statement of Communist ideology. (113)

In this study we are not so concerned with the political content of
Max's speech as we are with the fact that Wright chose to have the
defense attorney make a sociological rather than a legal argument on
Bigger's behalf.   Any weakness in Book Three is technical, not
ideological.   It stems from the fact that Wright has Max, not Bigger,
speak for Wright's political beliefs.   In Books One and Two we are
experiencing the world as Bigger lives it, but that world is limited in
its political views.   Bigger's involvement in the political system
consists of selling his vote for five dollars (Wright 331). Wright must
use someone else to represent the political activity that Wright sees as
one way for the blacks to escape their environment, and the espousal
of these political views through the defense attorney slows the pace of
the narrative:

> The tension relaxes and the pace slows in Book Three as the center of
> emphasis shifts somewhat from Bigger the individual to Bigger the social
> symbol. . . . The action of Book Three, Bigger's imprisonment and trial, is
> analytical, verbal, and psychological, not dramatic, physical, and psycholog-
> ical as in Books One and Two. (Kinnamon, *"Native Son"* 61)

Thematically in *Native Son* we once again see the outsider
struggling to survive in a system that ultimately is responsible for
deciding his guilt or innocence.   The prosecutor and the defense
counsel both have the traditional political motives explored in
Dreiser's text.   Here Wright has added the Communist cause that
motivates those representing Bigger.   The class element in *Native Son*
is both social class and economic class, and neither can be completely

separated from race. Bigger is poor, uneducated, and considered a
nonperson, even by the Daltons' white servant, Peggy: " 'He's just
like all the other colored boys. . . . He's just a quiet colored boy' "
(Wright 180). The only other people held in such low regard are the
Communists such as Jan, who is initially arrested for Mary's murder,
and the defense attorney, Max. Mr. Dalton's real estate company
owns the building in which Bigger, his mother, his brother, and his
sister rent one room for eight dollars a week. His defense for
charging more rent for a room in the Black Belt than in white sections
of town is the law of supply and demand. To charge any less would
be unethical because he would be underselling his (white) competitors
(Wright 50, 303–04). The issue of race permeates each of the other
issues. The police cordon off the Black Belt, accept the help of
vigilante groups, pick up several hundred blacks who resemble Bigger,
and use eight thousand men to search cellars, old buildings, and over
one thousand homes of blacks, presumably without warrants (Wright
228–29, 240). Bigger's killing of Mary Dalton is accidental while his
murder of Bessie is premeditated; yet even Bigger knows that he will
be punished for the accidental death because the victim is white
(Wright 306–07). Bigger is charged with the rape of Mary, although
there is no evidence of this crime, because that is what black men do
to white women.

Wright explores social issues in the same way Dreiser does: he
argues that if we keep blacks in this restrictive, unjust environment,
then we have only ourselves to blame if they strike out. According
to Margaret Walker, the thesis of *Native Son* is that "[t]he environment of a slum and the fear of crossing the white man's sexual and
civil laws bred young black criminals" (150). This analysis is similar
to the conclusion reached by Dreiser about the morally restrictive
environment in which Clyde was operating and which he could escape
only if sufficiently wealthy. In addition Keneth Kinnamon notes the
theme of rebellion throughout Wright's text, a theme we will see again
in Capote and Mailer (Kinnamon "*Native Son*" 67).

McWilliams argues persuasively that Wright does something very interesting with the legal terminology in the text:

> Wright selects a term associated with a legal condition, then redefines the term as a mental attitude that is a response to social conditioning, not individual will. This continuing process of redefinition serves to subordinate legal deed to psychological health as the valid standard of judgment. At certain moments, Wright is even led to the verge of condoning crime, as well as explaining it, on grounds of its psychological benefit. (102)

As an example of this redefinition, McWilliams cites the use of the term "murder":

> A plausible legal defense against the charge of murder might have been that Mary Dalton's death was an unpremeditated accident. Wright grants this traditional defense ("though he had killed by accident . . . ") but almost immediately shifts the meaning of the term: "And in a certain sense, he knew that the girl's death had not been accidental. He had killed many times before, only on those other times there had been no handy victim or circumstance to make visible or dramatic his wish to kill." (101)

McWilliams notes that Wright does a similar redefining of the term "rape." Bigger is accused of the rape of Mary, which he did not commit, but Wright leads the reader to believe Bigger is a "rapist in spirit" (McWilliams 101).

The legal process in *Native Son* is tailored very carefully to allow the strongest presentation of Wright's social and political arguments. Wright takes more artistic license with criminal procedure than Dreiser did, such as when he creates an administratively unrealistic jail cell visitation scene, an hour-long side bar conference, and an improbably short time span between inquest and trial. The major difference between the judicial process in Dreiser and what Wright does here is that, in order to have an effective forum for his arguments that are social, not legal, Wright has Bigger confess and plead guilty to the crime. The forum for Max's plea on behalf of Bigger thus becomes a sentencing hearing rather than a trial, the same strategy used by Clarence Darrow in the Leopold and Loeb case where Darrow managed to save the defendants' lives. Here is the chain of events: inquest, indictment by the grand jury, arraignment at which a plea of not guilty is entered, and a trial at which a guilty plea is entered and immediately followed by a sentencing hearing (Wright 336). These events comprise Book Three of the narrative and cover the last 138 pages, or thirty-five per cent, of the text.

The prosecutor is State's Attorney Buckley. In a foreshadowing technique employed by Wright throughout the narrative, Buckley is first introduced to the reader on page 16, where Bigger watches workmen putting up a billboard for Buckley's reelection campaign. Bigger notices how the eyes in the photograph of Buckley follow him as he walks away. The caption on the poster reads: "If you break the law, you can't win" (Wright 16). Later in his cell, Bigger recognizes Buckley. Buckley's political ambition is not lost on Jan and Boris Max:

> "What in hell you reds can get out of bothering with a black thing like that, God only knows," Buckley said, rubbing his hands across his eyes.
> "You're afraid that you won't be able to kill this boy before the April elections, if we handle his case, aren't you, Buckley?" Jan asked. (Wright 271)

The political positions and motivations of the attorneys are clear from their first confrontation in Bigger's cell.

Boris Max is variously described by readers as "the personification of a dialectical thesis rather than a fully characterized individual" and as an "idealized [portrait] of [a] selfless, noble, dedicated [striver] toward the new social order" (Grenander 225; Kinnamon, "Background" 71–72). Some critics accuse Max of opportunism, of using "his client for the Communist portrayal of American oppression," while others say there is no proof in the text that Max is a party member and he is instead "an old, wise, weary Jew, deeply aware of the radical defects of the society" (Grenander 226; Siegel 108). When evaluating the character Boris Max, one must distinguish between his function as a defense attorney in a death penalty case and his function as a proponent of Wright's thematic agenda. As a defense attorney, Max is ineffective. Bigger is executed, the ultimate failure. From a legal perspective, Hakutani is correct in stating that Bigger is "represented to his disadvantage" by Max. "A more convincing argument in that courtroom would have been for the defense to plead insanity rather than to demonstrate that Bigger is a victim of society" (Hakutani 217). As Holladay accurately assesses:

> Max is so caught up in his own windy rhetoric, in fact, that he ignores two glaringly obvious means of winning the case: pleading not guilty or pleading insane. The former plea would place the burden of proof on the prosecution, and the latter would at least give him the opportunity to recast Bigger's crimes in a different light. (35)

Max is, however, the perfect lawyer to support Wright's thematic agenda. Whether one views Max's motives as Communist opportunism or sympathetic but ineffective lawyering, Max is a catalyst of Bigger's self-understanding and an instrument of Bigger's death which in turn is Bigger's triumph of identity.

Wright admits the administrative improbability of the scene in Bigger's cell where Bigger is visited all at one time by a preacher, Jan, Max, Buckley, the Daltons, his mother, sister, brother, and three friends. "I felt that what I wanted that scene to say to the reader was *more important than its surface reality or plausibility*" (Wright's emphasis, "Bigger" 43). At the end of the scene, Bigger is alone in the cell with Buckley, who accuses Bigger of additional crimes and finally, by a combination of subtle threats and sympathy, induces him to confess to the murders of Mary and Bessie:

> . . . Buckley looked at the other white man [the stenographer] and smiled.
> "That was not as hard as I thought it would be," Buckley said.

"He came through like a clock," the other man said.

Buckley looked down at Bigger and said,

"Just a scared colored boy from Mississippi."

There was a short silence. Bigger felt that they had forgotten him already. Then he heard them speaking.

"Anything else, chief?"

"Naw. I'll be at my club. Let me know how the inquest turns out."
(Wright 287–88)

An inquest is "the inquiry by a coroner or medical examiner, sometimes with the aid of a jury, into the manner of the death of anyone who has been killed, or has died suddenly under unusual or suspicious circumstances, or by violence, or while in prison" (Nolan and Nolan-Haley 792). In the case of Mary Dalton the inquest is also to establish her identity since only ashes and pieces of bone remain. The inquest in this instance is conducted by the deputy coroner before a jury of six men. As with Dreiser, Wright is selective about who testifies and how much we hear each say. Mrs. Dalton testifies as to the family background and identifies by touch the heirloom earring worn by Mary and found in the ashes of the furnace. She describes the events of the night of her daughter's death as she remembers them and says that she and her husband have donated over five million dollars to black educational institutions. When her testimony is completed the deputy coroner has the jurors view the remains of the deceased, the pile of bones. Mrs. Dalton's testimony serves the same thematic purpose as the testimony of Roberta's father in *An American Tragedy*: to highlight the hostile feelings toward the accused being generated by an appeal to community standards such as the value of the family.

Jan testifies about his date with Mary that night. The deputy coroner asks questions about Jan's Communist activities, to which Max, although there to represent Bigger not Jan, objects:

"Mr. Coroner, I realize that this is not a trial. But the questions being

asked now have no earthly relation to the cause and manner of the death of
the deceased."

"Mr. Max, we are allowing plenty of latitude here. The grand jury will
determine whether the testimony offered here has any relation or not."

"But questions of this sort inflame the public mind . . . ."

"Now, listen, Mr. Max. No question asked in this room will inflame
the public mind any more than has the death of Mary Dalton, and you know
it. You have the right to question any of these witnesses, but I will not
tolerate any publicity-seeking by your kind here!" (Wright 296)

The deputy coroner's approach would be acceptable if he applied
these rules evenhandedly. As we shall see, he does not. He continues
to cut off any explanations that Jan tries to make, and he asks leading
questions that would appear to be beyond the scope of an inquest.
Yet when Mr. Dalton is questioned by Max about his real estate
holdings and the rent he charges, the deputy coroner steps in: " 'I'll
not tolerate your brow-beating this witness! Have you no sense of
decency? This man is one of the most respected men in this city!
And your questions have no bearing . . . ' " (Wright 302). Max is
able to continue only because Mr. Dalton volunteers to answer his
questions. "After Mr. Dalton left the stand, Peggy came, then Britten,
a host of doctors, reporters, and many policemen" (Wright 304). Max
indicates that Bigger does not wish to testify, as is his right. The
jurors examine the evidence, including the kidnap note, Mary's purse,
the blood-stained knife with which Bigger tried to decapitate Mary,
the blackened hatchet blade, the Communist pamphlets Jan had given
Bigger, the rum bottle discovered by the car, the trunk, and the signed
confession. The deputy coroner has one last piece of evidence,
however; to everyone's shock he has the "raped and mutilated" body
of Bessie Mears wheeled into the room. Max argues that the coroner
is now appealing to mob emotion and that all of the evidence he needs
on the death of Mary Dalton is contained in Bigger's confession, to
which the deputy coroner responds, " 'That's for the grand jury to
determine! . . . I have the legal right to determine what evidence is

necessary. . . . ' " (Wright 306). The jurors' decision is that Mary Dalton died of suffocation and strangulation after being "choked by the hands of one, Bigger Thomas, during the course of criminal rape," and they recommend he be held for the grand jury on a charge of murder (Wright 308). After the inquest Bigger is taken to the Daltons' home to reenact the crime, which he refuses to do. " 'You can't make me do nothing but die!' " (Wright 312).

Bigger, being held in the segregated Cook County Jail, asks to see a newspaper. He has already used the papers to follow the progress of the police hunt for him and to follow the progress of the case since he has been arrested. Wright's use of actual news stories as the basis for the newspaper accounts in the narrative was very important in hindsight. Readers might assume that Wright was guilty of gross exaggeration in his fictionalized newspaper clippings were it not for the fact that these stories are based on *Tribune* articles of 1938–39. Fabre alleges that Wright quoted word for word from the *Tribune* (172). The racism in what Bigger reads is frightening:

> "Though the Negro killer's body does not seem compactly built, he gives the impression of possessing abnormal physical strength. He is about five feet, nine inches tall and his skin is exceedingly black. His lower jaw protrudes obnoxiously, reminding one of a jungle beast. . . .
>
> "All in all, he seems a beast utterly untouched by the softening influences of modern civilization. In speech and manner he lacks the charm of the average, harmless, genial, grinning southern darky so beloved by the American people." (Wright 260)

Wright makes thematic use of the newspaper stories not only to record the racism of America in the 1930s, but also to demonstrate the presumption that Bigger is guilty. Bigger is labeled "the killer" in the excerpt quoted above rather than "the accused." The paper goes so far as to make an explicit determination of guilt that should be left to the legal process to decide: " '. . . slayer will undoubtedly pay supreme penalty for his crimes. . . . there is no doubt of his guilt. . . . What is doubtful is how many other crimes he has committed. . . .' " (Wright 316).

Wright reports the private discussions between Bigger and his attorney in great detail. One reason is to allow Bigger to tell his story out loud in his own words. Another reason is a practical one that Bigger recognizes later: Max is seeking facts about Bigger to use in his argument before the judge (Wright 333). A third reason is to highlight the fact that Bigger has finally found someone who will listen to him, even if Max cannot fully understand. Max asks the questions we might ask if we could speak to Bigger. (Webb points out that these questions are also the racist questions Buckley asks [174].) We want to know more about why he did what he did and how he feels. " 'I killed 'em 'cause I was scared and mad. But I been scared and mad all my life and after I killed that first woman, I wasn't scared no more for a little while' " (Wright 328). Max tries to explain to Bigger why Mary acted the way she did. Bigger responds, " 'White folks and black folks is strangers. We don't know what each other is thinking. Maybe she was trying to be kind; but she didn't act like it. To me she looked and acted like all other white folks. . . .' " (Wright 325). Max asks about Bigger's dreams for a career which were foreclosed by racism, about the black leaders who Bigger says would not listen to blacks like him, and about the South Side Boys' Club, where Mr. Dalton donated ping pong tables and Bigger and his friends planned their robberies (Wright 324–30). (Wright cites his own tenure at the real South Side Boys' Club as an event that prompted him finally to begin writing about all of the Biggers he had known [Wright, "Bigger" 39].) At the end of their discussion, Max advises Bigger to plead not guilty at the arraignment the next day but to plead guilty and ask for mercy at trial (Wright 331). Under the circumstances, Max may be right. Bigger has already refused to enter a plea of insanity. A not guilty plea before a jury would probably be no more successful in undermining the prosecutor's assertion of Bigger's intent to harm Mary than that plea was when Clyde argued lack of intent toward Roberta in *An American Tragedy*. The only hope is to have the right judge, someone sympathetic to sociological and psychological arguments.

Wright propels the action forward to the trial and indicates that from the end of the inquest to the trial only one week has passed, which would be an unrealistically short period of time in any court system (336). Before entering the courtroom, Bigger reads in the paper that the National Guard has been called out " 'to keep the public peace during the trial of Bigger Thomas, Negro rapist and killer' " (Wright 338). There is no unbiased reporting in *Native Son*.[4] In court Max coaches Bigger in a realistic and practical fashion.

> ". . . When the judge asks how you want to plead, say guilty."
> ". . . And let the judge see that you notice what's going on."
> "I hope Ma won't be there."
> "I asked her to come. I want the judge to see her," Max said.
> "She'll feel bad."
> "All of this is for you, Bigger."
> "I reckon I ain't worth it."
> "Well, this thing's bigger than you, son. In a certain sense, every Negro in America's on trial out there today." (Wright 340)

Bigger sees his mother, brother, sister, schoolmates, teachers, and friends in the audience.

Court is called to order, and Chief Justice Alvin C. Hanley calls the attorneys to the bench for a sidebar conference. A sidebar conference is a discussion, often on procedural matters or questions of law, between the judge and the attorneys held at the "side of the bar" beyond the hearing of the jury or the audience. A sidebar conference may be on or off the record; that is, the judge decides whether to have the court reporter record the discussion for the official transcript of the proceeding. After the conference is completed, Bigger's indictment is read and Max pleads Bigger guilty. Max then states that he would like to present evidence of Bigger's mental and emotional attitude in mitigation of punishment, and he would ask the court to consider the guilty plea itself in mitigation. Buckley objects, saying that Max cannot plead that Bigger is both guilty and insane, and asserts he will submit witnesses and evidence to establish Bigger's legal sanity.[5] "Max is therefore left in the weak position of arguing that, although Bigger is not 'legally insane,' his 'mental and emotional attitude' should mitigate his responsibility" (Grenander 227). There is a long argument, which Bigger does not understand, and then another sidebar conference, which lasts over an hour. Apparently the judge decides to hear testimony in aggravation and mitigation of punishment. Bigger is asked to stand, and the judge questions him on how far he went in school. The possible sentences—death, life in prison, prison for not less than fourteen years—are explained to Bigger by the judge, and he asks if Bigger understands the consequences of his guilty plea (Wright 341–44). Once Bigger answers in the affirmative, the plea is accepted and the prosecutor can proceed.

Buckley begins with a statement to the court, during which he says, " 'It is not often . . . that a representative of the people finds the masses of citizens who elected him to office standing literally at his back, waiting for him to enforce the law.' " The audience responds, " 'Kill 'im now!' " and " 'Lynch 'im!' " Max objects that Buckley is attempting to intimidate the court, the objection is sustained, and Buckley is admonished by the judge. Buckley apologizes, claiming his emotions got the best of him. Buckley uses several other tactics during his statement to make his point, such as threatening to resign if Bigger's life is spared and threatening to demand a jury trial if the defense continues to say Bigger is insane—which is not what Max is saying in the first place. When Max objects, Buckley counters with his own objection to Max's calling the defendant by anything other than the name in the indictment: " 'Such names as "Bigger" and "this poor boy" are used to arouse sympathy' " (Wright 347). The judge sustains the objection. Buckley's statement is over, and he tells the judge he has sixty witnesses to call.

Max reiterates that he is not saying that Bigger is insane: " 'I shall put no witnesses upon the stand. *I* shall witness for Bigger Thomas. I shall present argument to show that his extreme youth, his mental and emotional life, and the reason why he has pleaded guilty, should and must mitigate his punishment' " (Wright 348).   He cites the Leopold and Loeb case as an example of what he is trying to do, and he cites the law of Illinois that permits evidence in aggravation and mitigation of punishment: " 'The object of this law is to caution the Court to seek to find out *why* a man killed and to allow that *why* to be the measure of the mitigation of the punishment' " (Wright 348). When Max's statement is finished, the court adjourns.

Court reconvenes an hour later, and Buckley begins to call his witnesses: Mary's maternal grandmother; Mrs. Dalton, who repeats the story she told at the inquest; Mr. Dalton; Peggy, the housekeeper; Britten, the private investigator; fifteen newspapermen; five white men who identify Bigger's handwriting on the kidnap note; a man who identifies Bigger's fingerprints on the door of Mary's room; six doctors, who verify that Bessie was raped; four black waitresses from Ernie's Kitchen Shack, who identify Bigger as the dinner companion of Mary and Jan; two of Bigger's school teachers; Jan; Bigger's friends G. H., Gus, and Jack, who tell how the group stole; Doc from the pool hall, who tells how Bigger cut the cloth on the pool table; sixteen policemen, who identify Bigger as the man they captured; a juvenile court officer, who testifies that Bigger served three months in reform school for stealing tires; and five doctors, who state that Bigger is " 'sane, but sullen and contrary' " (Wright 350–51).   Wright presents the testimony of these witnesses in summary form, and the cumulative effect is that not only did Bigger commit the crimes to which he confessed, but that he was also involved in lesser crimes from a very young age. In addition, each of the non-expert witnesses with personal knowledge of Bigger testifies that he acted "sane." Max does not cross-examine the witnesses. His position is that this is a guilty plea proceeding, not a sanity hearing, but his failure to cross-examine may leave the judge with the impression that none of these witnesses can be challenged in any way (Wright 350). Finally, Buckley presents the physical evidence as he did at the inquest: the knife, purse, brick, flashlight, Communist pamphlets, gun, earring, hatchet blade, confession, kidnap note, Bessie's clothes, stained pillows and quilts, trunk, empty rum bottle, and Mary's bones. Just as Dreiser has the district attorney in *An American Tragedy* recreate the crime in the courtroom with the rowboat, so Wright has Buckley recreate the culmination of Bigger's crime. Buckley has the Daltons' furnace reconstructed in the courtroom:

> Buckley had a white girl, the size of Mary, crawl inside of the furnace "to prove beyond doubt that it could and did hold and burn the ravished body of innocent Mary Dalton; and to show that the poor girl's head could not go in and the sadistic Negro cut it off." (Wright 352)

After this demonstration, the state rests.

Max advises the court that he does not contest the evidence and waives the right to call witnesses. This waiver is yet another example of Max's ineffectiveness. As Holladay notes, "Max, for his part, would do well to bolster his defense by bringing in psychiatrists, social workers, and character witnesses" (31). After Buckley presents an hour's summation of his evidence, Max is entitled to present his plea on Bigger's behalf.[6]

Max's speech covers 17 pages of text, and it is Wright's opportunity to espouse his opinions on the causes of crime in the black community and the consequences of ignoring those conditions (Wright 353–70). "Wright frees Boris Max to direct the trial toward disclosure of the psychological and economic forces that cause thousands of Bigger Thomases to commit crime" (McWilliams 103). To McWilliams Max is speaking "as a criminologist whose assumptions about causation are fundamentally Marxist" (103). Max asserts that as a black criminal Bigger comes into court with a handicap " 'notwithstanding our pretensions that all are equal before the law,' " and we must try to understand the life of Bigger Thomas (Wright 354). Max speaks about the atmosphere surrounding a case into which " '[e]very conceivable prejudice has been dragged. . . . The hunt for Bigger Thomas served as an excuse to terrorize the entire Negro population, to arrest hundreds of Communists, to raid labor union headquarters and workers' organizations' " (Wright 356). Max also imputes motive for the state's methods:

> "Who, then, fanned this latent hate into fury? Whose interest is that thoughtless and misguided mob serving?
> "The State's Attorney knows, for he promised the Loop bankers that if he were re-elected demonstrations for relief would be stopped! The Governor of the state knows, for he has pledged the Manufacturers' Association that he would use troops against workers who went out on strike! The Mayor knows, for he told the merchants of the city that the budget would be cut down, that no new taxes would be imposed to satisfy the clamor of the masses of the needy!" (Wright 356–57)

This type of argument probably would not be permitted in court. Max is doing what he has accused Buckley of doing—making accusations, here about third parties, without proof, but Wright is making arguments that he feels obligated to make on behalf of all of the Biggers he has known.

Max states, " 'Fear and hate and guilt are the keynotes of this drama!' " (Wright 357). But Max wants to make it clear that he is not claiming that Bigger is a victim of injustice because the concept of injustice is premised upon equal claims. As McWilliams explains, "When social conditions wholly preclude equality, there can be no justice even if legal procedures are equitable" (104). Max pleads with the court " 'to see a mode of *life* in our midst, a mode of life stunted and distorted, but possessing its own laws and claims' " (Wright 358). Max reviews in detail the history of the black race as slaves, first to the farm and now to the machine. Out of this slave/master relationship comes the climate of this courtroom: " 'This guilt-fear is the basic tone of the prosecution and of the people in this case' " (Wright 360). Max asserts that what is happening under these circumstances is not injustice but oppression, " 'an attempt to throttle or stamp out a new form of life' " (Wright 360). Max believes, " 'The surest way to make certain that there will be more such murders is to kill this boy' " (Wright 361). Mary's death was accidental, but the feelings that motivated Bigger had been there a long time. To Bigger, this was not murder:

> "He was *living*, only as he knew how, and as we have forced him to live. The actions that resulted in the death of those two women were as instinctive and inevitable as breathing or blinking one's eyes. It was an act of *creation*!" (Wright 366)

As Holladay notes, many of Max's points are rhetorically flawed by generalization and logical fallacy (31–34). The conclusions he reaches, however, are compelling:

> "Your Honor, another civil war in these states is not impossible; and if the misunderstanding of what this boy's life means is an indication of how men of wealth and property are misreading the consciousness of the submerged millions today, one may truly come." (Wright 369)

Max pleads that Bigger's life be spared, that prison would be a better environment than that from which he has come. By sending Bigger to prison, " 'You would be for the first time conferring *life* upon him. . . . The other inmates would be the first men with whom he could associate on a basis of equality' " (Wright 369–70). Finally Bigger would have the basics on which the country was founded, " 'personality and security' " (Wright 370). Wright tells us, "[Bigger] had not understood the speech, but he had felt the meaning of some of it from the tone of Max's voice" (Wright 370). To the reader the defense attorney's speech includes recurring images and themes of the text, such as the themes of blindness and of killing as a route to freedom and the images of walls or curtains or veils and of the white world as a natural force (Siegel 110–12).

Wright modeled Max's argument on the plea used by Clarence Darrow in the Leopold and Loeb case. But those two defendants were wealthy and white. Is Wright suggesting that Darrow's daring sociological/psychological argument was effective because Darrow had "ideal" defendants? Or is it that Bigger lacks the funds for the extensive expert testimony on mental condition that was employed by Darrow? Either question leads to the same answer: being black and poor guarantees different treatment in the criminal justice system. Because he is "a product of American racism and capitalist greed," Bigger cannot win his legal case (Rampersad, Introduction 6).

Buckley opens his speech with a reminder that the judge is bound by the law, implying that the judge should not be swayed by sociological concerns: " 'Your Honor, we all dwell in a land of living law. Law embodies the will of the people' " (Wright 371–72). One assumes this communal will does not include marginal people like Bigger. Buckley asserts he is simply doing his duty and has no interest in the case beyond that duty. As far as Max's arguments go, Buckley will not dignify the " 'silly, alien, communistic and dangerous ideas' " with a response. " 'I know of no better way to discourage such thinking than the imposition of the death penalty upon this miserable human fiend, Bigger Thomas!' " (Wright 372). Buckley's argument is very carefully constructed, and he chooses to defuse the issues of race and class by accusing the defense of raising those issues. He says Max has " 'assailed our sacred customs' " and has a " 'deluded and diseased mind' " (Wright 373). Ironically, Buckley goes on to present stereotypical images of women and blacks:

"It is a sad day for American civilization when a white man will try to stay the hand of justice from a bestial monstrosity who has ravished and struck down one of the finest and most delicate flowers of our womanhood.

"Every decent white man in America ought to swoon with joy for the opportunity to crush with his heel the woolly head of this black lizard, to

keep him from scuttling on his belly farther over the earth and spitting forth
his venom of death!" (Wright 373)

Reilly attempts to put this racist speech in a historical context:

Exaggerated though Buckley's speech may appear today in its vicious
imagery and tone, in 1940 it was unexceptional, and in any case even if it
were presented in more cautious and acceptable rhetoric it would remain a
précis of the beliefs that justify the subordinate status of blacks as the
"other." (59)

Obviously, racial arguments this blatant are not permitted in our courts
today. We have become more sophisticated in the way we deal with
such racism. Prejudice still exists, but the appeal to that prejudice
must be more subtle or couched, as Reilly says, "in more cautious and
acceptable rhetoric."

Buckley continues his inflammatory tactics. He describes the
crime one more time in a slanted fashion, including the suggestion
that Bigger burned the body to hide crimes even worse than rape, such
as teeth marks on Mary's breast, of which there is no evidence. He
argues that Bigger planned the murder and tried to blame someone
else. It is interesting that when the state's attorney comes to the
killing of Bessie Mears, he must devise a way to make her a sympathetic victim. Here he falls back on class, not race, arguments,
describing Bessie as " 'that poor working girl' " (Wright 378).
Wright is emphasizing that as long as the blacks stay in their servile
roles, they too can be considered victims. But Buckley chooses to
spare the court the " 'ghastly details' " of the murders; he will let the
testimony of the witnesses speak for itself. Buckley argues that the
death penalty for Bigger will have a deterrent effect, a fact that has
never been proven in criminology, and will make people feel safe and
restore their confidence, which is probably true. In a twist on Max's
plea on Bigger's behalf, Buckley concludes, " 'Your Honor, in the
name of Almighty God, I plead with you to be merciful to us!' "

(Wright 379). While readers may deplore Buckley's tactics, he is merely fulfilling his role as the prosecutor. His job is to convict Bigger, and he uses appeals to prejudice effectively to accomplish that goal.

Max is horrified when the judge recesses for only one hour and promises his decision at the end of that time. He asks the judge to take more time, but the judge is adamant. Bigger declines to make a statement before sentence is passed. " 'In view of the unprecedented disturbance of the public mind, the duty of this Court is clear.' " The judge is apparently not persuaded by Max's argument that the "unprecedented disturbance" was caused by the prosecution, the police, and the press. "Such judicial pandering to popular racial prejudice reflects historical practice. . . . It was widely presumed that the stability of the court system could continue only as long as courts periodically acted out the retributive desires of the people" (McWilliams 105). The judge sentences Bigger to death. Max promises to see the Governor (Wright 380–81). Manfred Blake is correct as to Bigger's conviction for the death of Mary:

> Technically there has been a miscarriage of justice. The court has imposed the death penalty for a homicide in which there was no malice aforethought or accompanying crime [which would justify a felony-murder conviction]. . . . He had not raped her, as the State alleged. Nor was Bigger's subsequent conduct the confession of guilt that it seemed. Having suffocated the girl unintentionally, he cut off her head and stuffed her body into the furnace because of panicky fear. (M. Blake 234)

The fact remains that Bigger has killed Bessie in cold blood, and this murder makes his unjust conviction easier for the reader to accept. Wright ensures that this is not a case like Clyde Griffiths's in Dreiser's *An American Tragedy*, where intent is never clear and Clyde goes to his death for a murder of which he may not have been legally guilty.

Max's clemency appeal to the Governor fails. Bigger longs to speak once more to Max, the only man who ever really listened and tried to understand. Max arrives just hours before the execution. Bigger assures Max that he knows Max has done everything he could.

> "You asked me questions nobody ever asked me before. You knew that I was a murderer two times over, but you treated me like a man. . . . But sometimes I wish you hadn't asked me them questions. . . . They made me think and thinking's made me scared a little. . . . Mr. Max, how can I die!" (Wright 387–88)

" 'Men die alone, Bigger' " is the best response Max can manage. Bigger needs to talk, even if Max is uncomfortable listening under these sad circumstances. This is "a meeting of two men whom the American racial system has estranged from each other" (Reilly 59). Bigger admits he will be crying inside when they take him to the electric chair. He wants to know why people hated him so, whether they were just trying to get "something" like he was (Wright 388–89). Max then takes Bigger to the window that overlooks the skyline of Chicago:

> "The men who own those buildings are afraid. They want to keep what they own, even if it makes others suffer. . . . Bigger, the people who hate you feel just as you feel, only they're on the other side of the fence. . . . But on both sides men want to live; men are fighting for life. Who will win? Well, the side that feels life most, the side with the most humanity and the most men. That's why . . . y-you've got to b-believe in yourself, Bigger . . . ." (Wright 390–91)

Bigger laughs: " 'Ah, I reckon I believe in myself. . . . I ain't got nothing else. . . . I got to die . . . .' " (Wright 391). Bigger goes on to explain that, for him, killing was a way to feel, to become:

> "I didn't want to kill!" Bigger shouted. "But what I killed for, I *am*! It must've been pretty deep in me to make me kill! I must have felt awful hard to murder. . . ."

****

"What I killed for must've been good!" Bigger's voice was full of frenzied anguish. "It must have been good! When a man kills, it's for something. . . . I didn't know I was really alive in this world until I felt things hard enough to kill for 'em. . . . It's the truth, Mr. Max. I can say it now, 'cause I'm going to die. I know what I'm saying real good and I know how it sounds. But I'm all right. I feel all right when I look at it that way. . . ." (Wright 392)

Kathleen Gallagher sees as a predominant theme of Wright's fiction " 'that in a racist society blacks become criminals by virtue of their very existence' " (qtd. in C. Blake 192). "Bigger's crimes come to define who he is in the society which created him" (Friedland xxii).

Wright tells us that as Max listens to Bigger's speech Max's eyes are first full of terror, then full of tears. Bone suggests that what terrifies Max is that Bigger will die in hate (150). Bigger's attitude, rather than being one of hate, can instead be seen as one of resignation as to the imperfect society in which he lived. Max shakes Bigger's hand and says good-bye, but he cannot look at Bigger again. As Max walks away, Bigger calls out to reassure Max that he is all right, and asks Max to tell Jan that he said hello.

Bigger does not go to death hating all white men. He accepts the comradeship of Jan, for the first time in his life dropping the "mister" in front of a white man's name. But this comradeship he will extend only to those who have earned it in action . . . . (Siegel 115)

Caesar Blake's discussion of the commission of crime as a route to status focuses on the confrontation between Jan and Bigger after Bigger has confessed to killing Mary. This meeting "becomes the confrontation between the man whose property (and thus his status) has been appropriated and the man who has appropriated that property (and status) through crime. Is there any doubt that Bigger conceives of his crime as conferring status?" (C. Blake 195).

Several critics have noted that the outcome of the case is necessary to support Wright's theme of the outsider crushed by his conflict with the system but somehow stronger for the ordeal. "If Mr. Max had managed to win a life sentence for Bigger Thomas, he would have robbed him of his only claim to human courage and dignity" (Cowley 114). "The meaning for his life, which Max had thought to gain him the opportunity to build during life imprisonment, he had grasped from his recent experience under the duress of death" (Siegel 113). Wright appears to agree that Bigger's route to identity and dignity is through a clash with the system. "The most I could say of Bigger was that he felt the *need* for a whole life and *acted* out of that need; that was all" ("Bigger" 37).

Not much appears to have changed in the legal system between Dreiser's *An American Tragedy* and *Native Son*. More than fifty years after the publication of *Native Son*, Wright's narrative is still a vivid picture of the outsider trapped first in his environment and then in the system. The racism of today may have a more subtle texture, but it would be naive to suggest that it does not exist in a legal system run by human beings. The Communist principles in the text may be dated, but the disparity among the economic classes is probably as great now as it was in 1940, if not greater. Wright's themes of the effects of class and race on the individual remain fresh, and we still struggle to correct the flaws he highlighted in a legal process influenced by racism, politics, and greed. As we shall see in the works by Capote and Mailer, the flaws in the system remain but the senselessness of the crimes committed seems to increase. If anything, as we progress through the twentieth century, we as a society are even less able to deal with the types of criminals we are creating.

NOTES

1. Arnold Rampersad includes the following note on the Leopold-
Loeb case in the 1991 Library of America edition of *Native Son*.

> On May 21, 1924, Richard Loeb, an 18-year-old graduate of the
> University of Michigan, and Nathan Leopold, Jr., a 19-year-old graduate of
> the University of Chicago, both sons of wealthy businessmen, lured 14-
> year-old Robert Franks into their car, where Loeb murdered him with a
> chisel. After hiding the boy's naked body in a railway culvert, Loeb and
> Leopold sent Mr. Franks a ransom note demanding $10,000 for his son's
> safe return. Mr. Franks withdrew the money from his bank, but learned that
> his son's body had been found before the time appointed to drop the
> ransom from a railroad car. Investigators found a pair of spectacles with
> unusual horn rims near the body and traced them to Leopold. Under
> questioning both men confessed to the murder, which they said had been
> motivated by a desire to commit a perfect crime. They were defended by
> Clarence Darrow, who changed their plea from not guilty to guilty on July
> 21, 1924, and argued that their disturbed mental condition be accepted as
> a mitigating fact in determining their punishment. The state's attorney
> asked for the death penalty for both defendants, but on September 10 Judge
> John Caverly sentenced them to life imprisonment for the murder, plus 99
> years for the kidnapping. Loeb was killed by a fellow inmate in 1936;
> Leopold was paroled in 1958 and died in 1971. (932 note 571.20–26)

2. Keneth Kinnamon in "How *Native Son* Was Born" describes the
connection between the Nixon case, the actual case on which Wright's
narrative was based, and Bigger's use of the signature "Red."

> Chicago police used third-degree methods to extract from [Nixon]
> confessions, later withdrawn, of other crimes, including the murder of
> another woman a year earlier, in which he was alleged to have written the

words "Black Legion" with his victim's lipstick on her bedroom mirror. The Black Legion, as Humphrey Bogart fans will recall from a film about the group, was an extremist right-wing organization in Detroit and other Midwestern cities, a kind of Northern urban version of the Ku Klux Klan. When Bigger thinks of diverting suspicion from himself, he signs the ransom "Red" and draws a hammer and sickle. By changing from fascists to Communists, Wright implies that the latter share with Bigger the role of social outcast, a point Max emphasizes later in the novel. (214).

3.   Wright's agenda for his Chicago trip is included by Keneth Kinnamon in the notes to his chapter "How *Native Son* Was Born" in *Writing the American Classics*, edited by James Barbour and Tom Quirk:

1. Get detail map of the South Side. Street Car grades & maps
II. Pick out site for Dalton's home.
3. Get a good street layout for Dalton's home.
4. Select empty house for Bigger's murder of Bessie.
5. Trace with ample notes the legal route whch (sic) was taken in trying Nixon.
6. Go through Cook County Jail; get some dope from the project about it.
7. Get picture, if possible, and go through court where trial took place.
8. Select site for Blum's delicatessen.
9. Select area of Bigger's capture.
10. See, visit, death house at Stateville and talk to Nixon if possible.
11. Give Bessie's home a definite address.
12. (Detail execution, if possible (SEE).
13. Talk to ILD heads about pleas, court procedure. (Ira Silber)
14. Get from Chicago Public Library *Maureen's* book on Loeb and Leopold trial.
15. Get location of Loeb and Leopold and Franks old home.
16. Get other books from library pertaining to trial.
17. Investigate House of Correction for Boys.
18. Get complete dope on inquest.
19. Get a copy of inquest return verdict.
20. Get copy of indictments.

21. Get form in which judges (sic) sentence is rendered.
22. From what station would one go to Milwaukee on train?
23. Get "Old Rugged Cross" song for use in preacher's talk with Bigger.
24. Select site for Bigger's home (3700 block on Indiana). Investigate Indiana from 43 to 39 for scene of Bigger's capture. (228 note 12)

Wright's plans were obviously ambitious. There is no way to know exactly how much of this agenda was actually accomplished.

4. Apparently there was also no unbiased reporting in the Nixon case, on which the press material of *Native Son* is based. Keneth Kinnamon cites actual headlines in his article *"Native Son*: The Personal, Social, and Political Background": " 'Sift Mass of Clews for Sex Killer' " (68 note 10); " 'Brick Moron Tells of Killing 2 Women' " (71 note 24); " 'Science Traps Moron in 5 Murders' " (69 note 15); and " 'Brick Slayer is Likened to Jungle Beast' " (69 note 13). In his article Kinnamon includes an excerpt of this last story from the Chicago *Tribune* on which Wright based the news report on pages 260–61 in *Native Son*.

5. Arnold Rampersad's note to the Library of America edition of *Native Son* explains the applicable Illinois law and illustrates how that law was applied in the Leopold and Loeb case:

> Illinois law required that a plea of not guilty by reason of insanity be tried before a jury, which in the case of a conviction on a capital charge would then determine whether the defendant would receive the death penalty. If the defendant entered a guilty plea, however, punishment was set by the trial judge, who was required to weigh both aggravating and mitigating circumstances before passing sentence. In the Loeb and Leopold case, Clarence Darrow changed the defense plea to guilty because he thought a jury of twelve, with shared responsibility, would find it easier to impose the death penalty than a single judge would. He then presented extensive testimony by medical experts regarding Loeb and Leopold's

mental and physical condition, arguing that a combination of hereditary and environmental factors had disturbed their minds to the point where they bore diminished responsibility for their crimes. (Notes 933–34 note 797.34)

6. Arnold Rampersad, in an article in the *New York Times Book Review*, tells how Wright was encouraged to edit the version of *Native Son* that was ready for publication by Harper in 1939 in order to satisfy the Book-of-the-Month Club selectors, who wished to offer the text through the club. Wright agreed, and one of the areas to be edited was the speeches of the attorneys in Book Three ("Honest" 17). In 1991 The Library of America published the "restored" version of the text. Although the deletions do not appear substantial—and do not change our discussion of the trial process—Kinnamon lists some "interesting material" dropped from Book Three that had originally been part of the judicial process including: "the implicit comparison of Bigger to a fugitive slave," "anti-Semitism," "naive white liberalism," "social barriers between Bigger and Mary," "the analogy between black rebelliousness and the American Revolution," and "Bigger's sexuality" ("How Born" 209). If anything, these "restored" ideas serve to strengthen the argument that Wright saw the courtroom as a forum for sociological issues.

III

Truman Capote's *In Cold Blood*

By the time *In Cold Blood* was published in 1965, the issues of class and race raised by Dreiser and Wright were joined by a concern for the psychological aspects of the criminal and the use of the insanity defense in court. Hollowell, who compared *In Cold Blood* to *An American Tragedy* in its ability to describe a crime that epitomizes the age in which the crime occurred, notes the "social dislocations" of the sixties (85). Certainly in Perry Smith and Dick Hickock we see men estranged from their families and society in a way different from the experiences of Clyde and Bigger. These men are outsiders not only to the ruling class but even to their own group. Possibly this further estrangement is the reason why they commit senseless crimes, and why we search in vain for the motives for their actions.

Unfortunately, the debate about the style of Capote's self-described "nonfiction novel" has deflected critical attention from the many fine qualities inherent in his text. In an interview in the *New York Times Book Review* in January of 1966, when *In Cold Blood* was being released, Capote stated, " 'It seemed to me that journalism, reportage, could be forced to yield a serious new art form: the "nonfiction novel," as I thought of it' " (qtd. in Plimpton 2).[1] Capote also said that he transcribed the interviews that form the core of his narrative without the aid of on-the-scene note-taking or tape-recording and that he could achieve 95% accuracy by listening carefully and later writing down what he had heard (Plimpton 38).   As Gerald Clarke says in his biography of Capote, ". . . Truman did have a case, though it might have been better if he had let someone else make it for him" (359).   For our purposes we will use Plimpton's *New York Times Book Review* interview with Capote as a source of information about how he selected events from the actual crime on which *In Cold Blood* is based rather than as a springboard for further debate on journalism versus fiction writing.   Since the bulk of the criticism on *In Cold Blood* does, however, focus on this debate, a brief overview seems appropriate.

Galloway asserts that labeling the work as to genre is to some extent irrelevant:

> . . . it is worth observing that while *In Cold Blood* is certainly not a work of "fiction," neither is it a "documentary" in the conventional sense of the word. . . . [I]t is a careful and artful selection of details, calculated to evoke a variety of moods, to establish character, to produce suspense, and to convey a number of intricately related themes. (Galloway 155–56)

Galloway goes on to say that ". . . perhaps only a novelist would have seen the events in this manner . . ." (156).   But Alan Collett makes a persuasive argument that the label we choose may matter when it comes to how we evaluate the work because the same standards cannot be applied to nonfiction and fiction.   "Creativity involved in the selection and arrangement of true reports will be a different sort of creativity from that involved in creating a fictional (realistic) world" (Collett 289).

> If we insisted on reading *In Cold Blood* as a fictional account of real-life events we would condemn as crude precisely those examples of artistic creativity which we praise as "ironic" or "significant" when we read the novel as Capote says we should. (Collett 291)

Collett's argument is sound, but his position does not appear to exclude an appreciation for the "art" in what Capote has created.

Pizer, who uses the term "documentary narrative," gives his definition of art, and it directly applies to what Capote is doing: "By 'art' I mean that the author imposes theme upon the event portrayed by means of his selection, arrangement, and emphasis of the details of his documentation and of his narrative" (Pizer "Documentary" 106).

One critical camp supports the contention that Capote created a "work of art" (Tompkins 171; Garrett 12). Galloway sees the narrative as a major work of literature "for only a writer of exceptional talent could so skillfully have directed our attention to the larger issues which rest behind the 'facts' of this case" (162). Garrett goes so far as to argue that the claim of a new form called the nonfiction novel "may be blamed on the publisher and dismissed as a device" (91).

Other critics question the claim of the status of "literature" for the narrative—even while they sometimes praise the result. Diana Trilling says *In Cold Blood* is not a novel; "it is 'only' a book, a work of journalism of an exceptionally compelling kind" (254). "By his unwillingness to be implicated in his story . . . Mr. Capote is employing objectivity as a shield for evasion. This is what is resented" (Trilling 254). Trilling goes on to summarize the various categories of resentment. She asserts that some readers think Capote should have "thrown his weight to the Smith-Hickock side of the moral question"; others find Capote too sympathetic toward the murderers; some readers believe Capote's "unquestioning acceptance" of the townspeople and the authorities gives his implied assent to American society; others feel that Capote was the one writing in cold blood, "exploiting tragedy for personal gain" (Trilling 254). At least one critic is bothered by the fact that Capote is using the form to hide the weaknesses in the text:

> If you accuse Capote of distortion, he can plead the novelist's license; if
> you point out that Perry Smith's dreams of a poisonous diamond tree
> defended by a snake is [sic] lifted out of mythology and worse, parlor

Freud—or that godlike giant parrot is cribbed from Flaubert's *A Simple Heart*—his defense will be reportage: *the man said it.* (Yurick 158)

McAleer says, "Capote's nonfiction novel format kept him from sorting out his major theme from secondary ones"; in other words, Capote has no thesis (583). McAleer believes *In Cold Blood* pales in comparison to Dreiser's *An American Tragedy*. "*In Cold Blood*'s chief value then . . . may well be its affirmation . . . of the soundness of Dreiser's intuitions and methods" (McAleer 585). To Hollowell "Capote's role as a literary promoter is foremost" and that "His rhetoric of originality neglects to mention a whole tradition of true crime books he found it convenient to ignore . . ." (83). (It is ironic that Capote later makes the same claim of ingratitude toward predecessors about Mailer and himself [Grobel 113].) Kauffmann is especially vocal in his criticism of Capote: "What it all amounts to is the puffery of an artistically unsuccessful writer of fiction pursuing his love of the Gothic . . . into life" (Kauffmann 21).

What is important for our purposes is that Capote used a process of selection to form his narrative. Capote acknowledged this process:

> "I make my own comment by what I choose to tell and how I choose to tell it. It is true that an author is more in control of fictional characters because he can do anything he wants with them as long as they stay credible. But in the nonfiction novel one can also manipulate: if I put something in which I don't agree about I can always set it in a context of qualification without having to step into the story myself to set the reader straight." (qtd. in Plimpton 38)

Capote had been searching for some time for the right subject matter for his foray into creative journalism. In November of 1959, he read a brief article in the *New York Times* captioned " 'Wealthy Farmer, 3 of Family Slain' " (Clarke 317).

". . . after reading the story it suddenly struck me that a crime, the study of one such, might provide the broad scope I needed to write the kind of book I wanted to write. Moreover, the human heart being what it is, murder was a theme not likely to darken and yellow with time.

"I thought about it all that November day, and part of the next; and then I said to myself: Well, why not *this* crime? The Clutter case." (qtd. in Plimpton 3)

Capote sold his idea for a story to *The New Yorker*, enlisted the help of his friend the novelist Harper Lee as a research assistant, and one month after reading the newspaper account was in Kansas (Clarke 318–19). Clarke suggests that Capote's original interest in the Clutter case was not with the murderers, who had yet to be identified and captured, but with the effect of the crime on the community (319). When he began the project, Capote had no way of knowing that it would take six years to complete, would lead to personal involvement with the murderers, and would end with his attendance at their hangings.

In his *New York Times Book Review* interview Capote tells us that " 'My files would almost fill a whole small room, right up to the ceiling.' "

"All my research. Hundreds of letters. Newspaper clippings. Court records—the court records almost fill two trunks. There were so many Federal hearings on the case. One Federal hearing was twice as long as the original court trial." (qtd. in Plimpton 43)

Capote conducted interviews with the townspeople and the authorities in charge of the case during his first visit to Kansas in December 1959. By the time Dick and Perry were arrested, Capote had finished the original article he had conceived about the reaction of a small town to a multiple murder. He returned to Kansas, however, to see the defendants brought back for their arraignment in early January 1960 (Clarke 324).

> When Perry sat down in front of the judge to be arraigned, Truman
> nudged Nelle [Harper Lee]. "Look, his feet don't touch the floor!" Nelle
> said nothing, but thought, "Oh, oh! This is the beginning of a great love
> affair." In fact, their relationship was more complicated than a love affair:
> each looked at the other and saw, or thought he saw, the man he might
> have been. (Clarke 326)

Capote now had a more important story than even he had imagined. Eventually he would interview and correspond with the defendants and gather a total of 4,000 pages of notes (Clarke 331).

In Cold Blood is the story of the deaths of the Clutters and the lives of the murderers following the crime. Part I, "The Last to See Them Alive," opens in the village of Holcomb, Kansas, and describes the events on the Clutter farm on the last day of the lives of Herbert Clutter, 48, his wife, Bonnie, 45, and their two children, Nancy, 16, and Kenyon, 15 (Capote 15–17). This plot line is alternated with chapters describing the events of the same day in the lives of the murderers, Dick Hickock, 28, and Perry Smith, 31, both former inmates of Kansas State Penitentiary. (Pizer labels this a "dual sequential narrative" ["Documentary" 113].) The two groups of characters meet that night at the Clutter farm, where Dick has been told by a former cellmate that he will find a safe filled with money (Capote 58). We do not find out exactly what happens that night until the murderers confess, but we witness the discovery of the bodies and the beginnings of the investigation of the crime by Alvin Dewey, 47, the Kansas Bureau of Investigation's representative in Garden City, Finney County (Capote 96). We also view the reaction of the community to the deaths of four members of one of its leading families. The only physical evidence of any significance is a single bloody footprint (Capote 81).

After the Clutter murders, the alternating pattern of the text continues in Part II, "Persons Unknown," as we watch Al Dewey and the townspeople in the aftermath of the crime and we travel with Dick and Perry on a cross-country odyssey. The two strands intertwine in

Part III, "Answer," when Dick and Perry are arrested with the incriminating boots in their possession on December 30, 1959 in Las Vegas. The police use a typical ploy with the defendants: they suggest to each one that the other has confessed. Eventually both give statements, and what occurred in the Clutter house is revealed. There is some disagreement about who actually committed which murder—at first Perry says Dick killed the two women while Dick blames Perry for all four deaths, but Perry later claims to have killed all four people, and Dick is more than willing to go along with this version (Capote 277, 287). Both versions are testified to at trial by Alvin Dewey, who heard Perry's confession. Perry's final story is that, after tying up the victims and separating the men from the women, the defendants discovered there was no money in the house. They stole only Kenyon's radio, a pair of binoculars, and about forty dollars (Capote 272, 278). But when Dick hesitated about leaving " '*No* witnesses,' " as he had continually bragged, Perry took over, first cutting Herb Clutter's throat, then shooting him in the head, and finally systematically shooting Kenyon, Nancy, and Bonnie in the head with Dick's twelve-gauge shotgun (Capote 49, 276–77). In Part IV, "The Corner," the nickname for the execution site, the defendants are tried, found guilty, and sentenced to death. After a lengthy appeal process, they are hanged on April 14, 1965 (Capote 378–82).

This brief overview of the major events of the narrative obviously does not account for the style in which Capote conveys the information, and Capote's techniques enrich the text. It is true that Capote employs "a conventional four-part classical structure," but with a difference (Garrett 3). There are eighty-five scenes ranging in length from two paragraphs to twenty-five pages (Hollowell 72). "The narrative reads 'like a novel' largely because of the use of scene-by-scene reconstruction instead of historical narration, the ironic heightening of dialogue, and the skillful manipulation of point of view" (Hollowell 70). Pizer notes that about half of the text consists of direct quotation "in the form of monologue, dialogue, or snatches

of conversation within authorial comment and summary narrative"
("Documentary" 111–12).

We gain insight into the characters through flashbacks. We learn
about the Clutters, the perfect family to the casual observer but
somehow flawed. Mrs. Clutter is described as " 'nervous' " and she
suffers from " 'little spells' " that periodically require her hospitaliza-
tion (Capote 17). Because of her mother's condition and the absence
of her two older sisters, one married and one engaged, Nancy has to
take over many of the household duties. Mr. and Mrs. Clutter sleep
in separate rooms. Galloway finds:

> [T]here is something almost compulsive about the Clutters' good works,
> their cherry-pie public spirit and unimpeachable respectability . . . not that
> the Clutters seem too good to be true, but that their own standards seem to
> place such ferocious demands on the individual, and to ask him to perform
> in an uncompromisingly public arena. (Galloway 158)

Trilling believes "the most interesting aspect of Mr. Capote's book as
an American story lies . . . in the curiously ambiguous personality of
Mr. Clutter":

> One is reluctant . . . to draw so exemplary a citizen, a successful teetotaling
> Republican devout progressive farmer, into the circle of self-alienated
> Americans. Yet manifestly this was a man without connection with his
> inner self, living by forced intention, by conscious design, programmatical-
> ly, rather than by any happy disposition of natural impulse. (Trilling
> 258–59)

In other words, he did all the right things but he didn't enjoy them.

Through flashbacks we learn that both Dick and Perry have been
physically deformed in accidents. Dick was in a car accident in 1950.
"It was as though his head had been halved like an apple, then put
together a fraction off center. . . . the left eye being truly serpentine,
with a venomous, sickly-blue squint . . ." (Capote 43). Perry's
injuries, acquired in a motorcycle accident in 1952, are more serious:

". . . his chunky, dwarfish legs, broken in five places and pitifully scarred, still pained him so severely that he had become an aspirin addict" (Capote 43). We learn that Dick comes from a farming family, has been divorced twice and fathered three sons, and has earned a living as an auto mechanic when he is not stealing (Capote 34–35, 311–14). Perry is one of four children of a father of Irish descent and a Cherokee mother. The couple performed in rodeos until the mother's drinking became debilitating, and when the parents separated the children were placed in various homes. Perry is a bedwetter who was beaten by the nuns at the orphanage for his habit. After running away, he spent some time with his father in Alaska before joining the Merchant Marines at sixteen, and later joined the army, serving in Korea. He ended up in prison for a burglary (Capote 26–27, 309–11).

Many critics note the similarity between the themes of *An American Tragedy* and *In Cold Blood*, some explicitly, like McAleer, and others implicitly. "[T]he community is outraged not so much by the murders as by the assault on the American Dream which the murders signify" (McAleer 579). "Capote represents Hickock and Smith as moral perversions of decent men brought about by the poverty, violence, and ill-luck that reached back for at least one generation" (Reed 107). Galloway asserts "one unifying theme—the metamorphosis of dream into nightmare" (162). Capote clearly delineates the difference between the classes:

> The aristocracy of Finney County had snubbed the trial. "It doesn't do," announced the wife of one rich rancher, "to seem curious about that sort of thing." Nevertheless, the trial's last session found a fair segment of the local Establishment seated alongside the plainer citizenry. (339)

Capote also examines the idea of isolation or loneliness, "the strange isolation of human beings who become victims of an impersonal, often fearful agency" (Morris 177). Perry becomes "the total symbol for the exile, the alienated human being, the grotesque, the outsider, the quester after love, the sometimes sapient, sometimes innocent, sometimes evil child" (Morris 186). Christensen notes that Perry and Dick do at first form a relationship, at least in their propensity for violence. "Despite Capote's denial of homosexual attraction between the team of murderers, here we have a chilling example of men who exert what is perhaps a fatal influence over each other in the course of their bonding" (Christensen 54). In addition to the themes that Capote shares with the other authors we have discussed, Hellmann refers to "the mythic theme of paradise lost" and "a parable of innocence destroyed," and McAleer cites the thematic elements of violation of "the mythic Garden of the World" and "estrangement from Nature" (Hellmann 67; McAleer 575). Herb Clutter's remark " 'an inch more of rain and this country would be paradise—Eden on earth' " supports the views of both Hellmann and McAleer (Capote 15–24).

What makes Capote's work different from that of Dreiser, Wright, and Mailer is that Capote attended the actual trial and took his own notes on the proceedings. He does not depend on newspaper articles or secondhand notes when he recreates the trial. Capote admitted that " 'the single most difficult thing in my book, technically, was to write it without ever appearing myself, and yet, at the same time, create total credibility' " (qtd. in Plimpton 38). Phillip K. Tompkins has written the most comprehensive article on the issue of what went on in the legal process, although his intention was to apply journalistic standards to Capote's text to discover if the facts were "true" (125). The trial process in *In Cold Blood* covers 61 pages, sixteen per cent of the text (Capote 283–344). This figure does not include the lengthy appeals process, which occupies the last 39 pages of the narrative. The actual trial transcript is only 515 pages long (Tompkins 127). Kauffmann alleges that the account of the trial is not "sufficiently interesting" to justify its length (19). One wonders what his opinion would be of the trial in *An American Tragedy*.

In Part IV, "The Corner," Capote begins the trial process with an entry from Perry's diary: *"Monday 11 January. Have a lawyer. Mr. Fleming. Old man with red tie"* (Capote 289). The arraignment has already occurred, but Capote has chosen to describe only the defendants' entrance into the Finney County courthouse at the end of Part III. We now learn that the defendants have pled insufficient funds and the court has appointed two lawyers to represent them. Neither lawyer wants the job. Perry's attorney, Arthur Fleming, 71, former mayor of Garden City and "a classic country lawyer more happily at home with land deeds than ill deeds," states, " 'I do not desire to serve . . . . But if the court sees fit to appoint me, then of course I have no choice' " (Capote 289, 318). Dick's lawyer, forty-five-year-old Harrison Smith, a golfer and an Elk who must assume an aggressive manner in court because "really he is a mild and lenient man," is equally unenthusiastic: " 'Someone has to do it. And I'll do my best. Though I doubt that'll make me too popular around here' " (Capote 289–90, 319). Mr. Smith appears at least as much concerned with his reputation in Garden City as with his client's best interests.

On the other hand, the county attorney, Duane West, is more enamored of the case. He is described as "an ambitious, portly young man of twenty-eight who looks forty and sometimes fifty" (Capote 290). Tompkins criticizes Capote's presentation of West because Tompkins believes that ". . . West is made to appear somewhat lower in rank than a law clerk" (Tompkins 170). Though Tompkins is correct that Capote does not tell us about West's role in the case, what Tompkins's assessment does not take into consideration is that the lawyers do not play as major a role in Capote's narrative as they do in *An American Tragedy* and *Native Son*.[2] Capote chooses to focus on the defendants rather than the lawyers. West, Fleming, and Smith all receive less attention than the lawyers in the other three narratives.

It is interesting that Dick, in his own version of events at trial, discusses one lawyer's trick that West uses—and reveals how effective the tactic is:

I never did think much of the Finney County Attorney and I sure liked him less after our first day in court. He kept pointing his finger at me and telling the jury how no good I was. I resented it. It wasn't so much what he was saying but how he was saying it and who he was saying it in front of.

*****

Every time the county attorney pointed his finger at me I wanted to hit him. (Hickock 82)

West plans to seek the death penalty because of the violence of the crime, the lack of mercy shown by the defendants, and in order to protect the public (Capote 290). West believes the death penalty is especially necessary under the circumstances considering that " 'in Kansas there is no such thing as life imprisonment without possibility of parole. Persons sentenced to life imprisonment actually serve, on the average, less than fifteen years' " (Capote 290). West appeals to the feelings of retribution and the fears of the public in calling for the death penalty.

The state has hired Logan Green as special assistant to Duane West:

Green, a suavely tough little septuagenarian, has an imposing reputation among his peers, who admire his stagecraft—a repertoire of actorish gifts that includes a sense of timing acute as a night-club comedian's. An expert criminal lawyer, his usual role is that of defender, but in this instance the state had retained him as a special assistant to Duane West, for it was felt that the young county attorney was too unseasoned to prosecute the case without experienced support. (Capote 339–40)

(Tompkins states that Green was retained at West's request rather than being forced on West as a partner [170].)

The judge is Roland H. Tate:

[A]s a fellow jurist once remarked, "Tate is what you might call a lawbook lawyer, he never experiments, he goes strictly by the text"; but the same critic also said of him, "If I were innocent, he's the first man I'd want on the bench; if I were guilty, the last." (Capote 301)

Capote is careful to include details about the judge that highlight his position as the archetypal "insider." He is rich, raises horses, and owns lots of land (Capote 298).

Capote's descriptions of the participants and the events in court are interspersed with the daily events of life in jail for Dick and Perry. The attorneys confer with their clients and discuss the possibility of a change of venue, the same issue raised in Dreiser's *An American Tragedy* (McAleer 574). Fleming advises Perry that he is just as well off in Garden City, which is a religious community and where most of the ministers are opposed to capital punishment, including the Clutters' own minister. Fleming is practical. " 'Remember, all we can hope is to save your lives' " (Capote 300).

The lawyers had already filed a pretrial motion shortly after the arraignment requesting a psychiatric examination for the defendants at the state hospital one hundred miles from Garden City to determine whether they were " 'insane, imbeciles or idiots, unable to comprehend their position and aid in their defense' " (Capote 300). The motion is opposed by Logan Green, who argues that Kansas law follows the M'Naghten Rule—whether the accused knew the nature of his act and knew it was wrong—and that nothing in the Kansas statutes requires that a psychiatrist determine competency; an ordinary doctor in Garden City would do. Smith argues in response that there are lives at stake here and that the defendants " 'are entitled to examination by persons of training and experience' " (Capote 301). The judge appoints a commission of three Garden City doctors to examine the defendants. After an hour's conversation with the defendants, the doctors rule that neither man suffers from a "mental disorder" (Capote 302). A second pretrial motion, this time for a delay of trial, is based on two factors, first, that Dick's father, a witness, is too ill to testify (he is dying of cancer) and second, that the estate auction at the Clutter farm is scheduled to be held the day before the trial begins and advanced publicity for the auction might influence the prospective jurors.   The judge denies the motion "without comment" (Capote 302–03).   (It would turn out that the attorneys were correct about the attraction of the auction—over five thousand people attended [Capote 303].)

The trial process begins with jury selection on March 22, 1960. Capote notes how "self-aware" the major participants are—all four lawyers wear new suits, and even Dick looks respectable in clothes provided by his family.   Only Perry is not properly dressed for the occasion; he wears a shirt borrowed from the undersheriff and jeans with the cuffs rolled up (Capote 306).   Capote goes into more detail about the jury selection process than Dreiser does.   We know that the jury pool is all male, that jury selection takes only four hours, that the twelve jurors and two alternates are selected from the first fifty-four questioned, that seven are rejected on preemptory challenges by the defense and three by the prosecution, that twenty are released because they either oppose capital punishment or have already formed an opinion about the case, and that the defendants are too busy writing statements for a psychiatrist who volunteered to examine them to pay much attention to jury selection.   (We eventually discover that Dick was paying attention.   He later wrote his own account of jury selection: "Our trial was more like a circus than anything else.   It took only one day to choose the jury.   The way the feeling was running around town I figured it would take at least three or four days for this. But the whole trial didn't last much longer than that" [Hickock 82].) The jury is ultimately composed of "half a dozen farmers, a pharmacist, a nursery manager, an airport employee, a well driller, two salesmen, a machinist, and the manager of Ray's Bowling Alley. They were all family men (several had five children or more), and were seriously affiliated with one or another of the local churches" (Capote 306–07).   Though Capote does not fully describe the questioning of potential jurors, he does provide some examples that highlight possible biases on the part of the jurors:

> During the *voir dire* examination, four of them told the court they had been personally, though not intimately, acquainted with Mr. Clutter; but upon further questioning, each said he did not feel this circumstance would hinder his ability to reach an impartial verdict. The airport employee . . . said, when asked his opinion of capital punishment, "Ordinarily I'm against it. But in this case, no"—a declaration which, to some who heard it, seemed clearly indicative of prejudice. [He] was nevertheless accepted as a juror. (Capote 307)

Presumably Capote was one "who heard it" and correctly assumed that this juror, who had already made up his mind about what kind of case this was, would be dismissed. It would seem advisable for defense counsel to challenge for cause the potential jurors who knew the Clutters, even if only slightly, especially when only fifty-four out of a panel of approximately one hundred and sixty had been questioned (Capote 306). Besides pointing out the possible bias of the jurors, a matter that can later be raised on appeal, Capote is also alerting the reader to the composition of the jury and emphasizing the position of Perry and Dick as outsiders in this community.

As the trial begins, the defendants "affected a courtroom attitude that was simultaneously uninterested and disinterested; they chewed gum and tapped their feet with languid impatience as the state summoned its first witness" (Capote 315). What is noteworthy here is not only that Capote focuses on the reactions of the defendants, as Dreiser focuses on Clyde's reactions and Wright on Bigger's reactions, but also that Capote fails even to mention the opening statements of the attorneys. He moves right from the defendants' courtroom behavior to the first witnesses for the state. As stated previously, the defendants are the object of Capote's attention, not the lawyers. What the lawyers have to say is not as important as the reactions of Perry and Dick.

Capote summarizes the testimony of all of the witnesses. In some cases we do hear brief exchanges between a witness and a lawyer, but we do not get extensive portions of question-and-answer. Testifying for the state concerning events on the morning after the murders are Nancy Ewalt and Susan Kidwell, who were first to enter the house; Nancy Ewalt's father; Sheriff Robinson; and the coroner, Dr. Fenton. Capote's method of summarizing testimony moves the narrative forward rapidly and makes the outcome appear inevitable. The defense waives cross-examination of each of these witnesses (Capote 315). This is probably an appropriate tactic because to question these witnesses will only emphasize the horror discovered in the house. Next to testify is Chief Investigator Rohleder, who took the crime scene photographs and identifies those photos on the stand. The prosecution offers the photos into evidence; the defense objects that the pictures are prejudicial and will inflame the jury. The judge overrules the objection, and the seventeen photographs, including pictures of the bodies, are shown to the jury. "It amazed them, it made them angry, and several of them . . . stared at the defendants with total contempt" (Capote 316). Dick's father comments to a journalist—Capote?—that the judge is prejudiced: " 'Just no sense having a trial' " (Capote 316). (Mr. Hickock mistakenly believes that the judge was a pallbearer at the Clutter funeral.)

The prosecution's final witness for the day is the "mystery man" who supplied the information that led to the arrest of the defendants. Floyd Wells, Dick's former cellmate, once told Dick about the Clutter farm and its alleged safe. As a state's witness, he was moved from the prison for his own safety, and he is "wearing a very decent dark-blue suit which the State of Kansas had bought for the occasion—the state being concerned that its most important witness should look respectable, and consequently trustworthy" (Capote 317). Capote is illuminating a common practice: looks count in court, and most attorneys advise clients on appearance and courtroom demeanor. The advice given to the prosecution's star witness is in contrast to the lack of attention paid to Perry's courtroom attire as described earlier. Capote notes another usual procedure: that Wells has been prepared for his time on the witness stand, his testimony "perfected by pretrial rehearsal" (Capote 317). Logan Green conducts the direct examination of Wells, who says he worked as a hired hand for the Clutters and, ten years later, discussed the family with Dick when they shared a cell in prison. Wells's testimony, as that of a key witness, is partially presented by Capote in question-and-answer form. Wells says he thought there had been a safe at the Clutters:

> "The next thing I knew he [Hickock] was talking about robbing Mr. Clutter. . . . He told me if he done anything like that he wouldn't leave no witnesses. . . . He told me he would probably tie them up and then rob them and then kill them." (Capote 318)

Capote is right; the state has "established premeditation of great degree" (Capote 318). During cross-examination Fleming implies that Wells should have done something if he believed Dick was serious. Wells responds that people are usually just talking in prison: " 'I didn't believe he'd do it.' " If that is so, then Fleming wants to know why Wells thought Dick had committed the crime. " 'Because it was done just like he said he was going to do!' " (Capote 318–19). Not a very successful cross-examination. Harrison Smith fares better when he questions Wells on behalf of Dick. He attacks Wells's credibility, asking whether Wells has a nickname like "Squealer" or "Snitch," which Wells denies. He asks how many times Wells has been in jail. Then he wants to know why Wells waited several weeks before telling his story to the authorities. Smith manages to get Wells to admit that a reward of one thousand dollars had been offered by a newspaper—and Wells had seen the paper—before Wells came forward. But the defense is stymied on the issue of immunity:

> "What kind of immunity did the county attorney offer you for coming up here today and testifying?"

. . . Logan Green protested: "We object to the form of the question,
Your Honor.   There's been no testimony about immunity to anybody."
(Capote 320)

The objection is sustained, and Wells is excused. Smith, in attempting
to show potential bias on Wells's part, was asking a question beyond
the scope of cross-examination. In some trials the prosecutor himself
raises the issue of immunity by asking the witness whether he has
been promised anything in exchange for his testimony. Here that
question was never asked on direct—possibly because the state did
suggest that something might be done for Wells—which makes the
topic of immunity "beyond the scope" of cross-examination. As
Wells leaves the stand, Dick comments, " 'Sonofabitch. Anybody
ought to hang, he ought to hang. Look at him. Gonna walk out of
here and get that money and go scotfree' " (Capote 320). And Capote
tells us Dick is right: ". . . not long afterward Wells collected both
the reward and a parole." And, also predictably, Wells eventually
ends up serving a thirty-year sentence for armed robbery in Mississippi (Capote 320).

The remaining prosecution witnesses represent law enforcement
agencies. Four Special Agents from the F.B.I., who are lab techni-
cians, testify concerning the physical evidence: "blood samples,
footprints, cartridge shells, rope and tape" (Capote 321). Four Kansas
Bureau of Investigation (K.B.I.) agents testify about the interviews
with the defendants and their confessions. On cross-examination the
defense attorneys attempt to show that the confessions were obtained
through coercion. "The allegation, which was untrue, irritated the
detectives into expounding very convincing denials" (Capote 321).
Here the lawyers' frustration is showing; they are damned if they do
nothing, but in fact there is nothing they can do. When a reporter
asks Smith why he pursued this particular line of questioning he responds, " 'What am I supposed to do? Hell, I'm playing without any
cards. But I can't just sit here like a dummy. I've got to sound off

once in a while' " (Capote 321).

Alvin Dewey is the state's most effective witness (Capote 321). Saving the strongest witness for last is usually a good idea because jurors tend to remember best what they hear last. Dreiser used this tactic when he had the prosecution's best evidence, Roberta's letters, read at the end of the prosecution case. Dewey testifies as to Perry's confessions because Perry ultimately refused to sign a statement. Tompkins asserts that Capote's version of the two confessions does not agree with the version published in the newspapers: "The two versions differ in many small details, but the most serious discrepancy concerns the mental state of Smith at the moment of the murder" (Tompkins 167). (Tompkins does an extensive review of the matter in his article.)   Capote, focusing as he does on the defendants' reactions in court, notes that this is the first time that Dick hears that Perry told the police that Dick intended to rape Nancy until Perry stopped him. This is also when Dick learns that Perry originally stated that Dick killed the two Clutter women, but later changed his story to accept responsibility for all four deaths. Dewey says, " 'He told me that Hickock . . . didn't want to die with his mother thinking he had killed any members of the Clutter family. And he said the Hickocks were good people. So why not have it that way' " (Capote 322). Perry's assertion that he was trying to spare the Hickocks is believable within the context of Capote's complex portrait of Perry. As we have already seen with Dick's father, Capote often records the response of those in the audience during the trial. Mrs. Hickock's response to this testimony is to cry. She says later that it was wrong of her to hate Perry, that she prays for Dick and Perry and the Clutters (Capote 323).

The defense case takes only ninety minutes during which five witnesses testify. The defendants do not testify in their own defense, "and therefore the question of whether Hickock or Smith had been the actual executioner of the family did not arise" (Capote 328). Capote is correct that unless the defendants testify as to their roles in the crime, the issue of individual responsibility cannot be explored. Only they know the truth. But Capote should have made clear that it does not matter, from a legal standpoint, who pulled the trigger. Under the Felony-Murder Rule in effect in Kansas at the time, and in many states today, one is responsible for any death that occurs during the commission of a felony in which one participates, such as a robbery. Whether a participant pulls the trigger or not is immaterial. The purpose of the rule is to emphasize the seriousness of participation in a felony—and to encourage would-be felons to choose their friends carefully. The criminal has no opportunity after the fact to argue "Not me." Apparently there was always disagreement over whether Dick actually killed anyone that night. Tompkins tells us that Duane West and Dewey both believed Dick had killed the women and adds: "[I]t was poor reporting to lead such a careful reader as Rebecca West [who mistakenly assumed Dick was unjustly executed since he had not actually shot anyone (113)] to the confident conclusion that Smith had committed all the Clutter murders while the principals were less than unanimous" (Tompkins 170). In addition to the lack of any method of assessing individual responsibility, it should also be noted that Dick might have fared better if the defendants had been tried separately. If Perry were willing to testify at Dick's trial that he, Perry, had killed the Clutters, then Dick would have a chance to argue for a life sentence rather than the death penalty. He would still be found guilty, but he would have a stronger case for sparing his life.

Dick's father, the first defense witness, does try to mitigate his son's responsibility by asserting that Dick has never been the same since his car crash in 1950. This testimony might hold some sway over the jury except for the fact, as prosecutor Green elicits on cross, that Dick was first arrested in 1949, *before* his accident, for breaking into a drugstore. The dialogue between Green and Mr. Hickock would be amusing were it not that poor Mr. Hickock, dying of cancer, is trying to do what little is within his power to help Dick:

". . . now you tell us your son had a change in his attitude and conduct after 1950?"

"I would say so, yes."

"You mean that after 1950 he became a *good* boy?"

*****

". . . He just didn't act like the same boy."

"You mean he *lost* his criminal tendencies?" (Capote 329)

Testifying next is Dr. W. Mitchell Jones, the psychiatrist who volunteered to examine the defendants when the court ordered a panel of local doctors, not psychiatrists, to rule on the defendants' mental condition. Under the M'Naghten Rule, he may be asked only if he has formed an opinion whether or not Dick knew the difference between right and wrong at the time of the commission of the crime. Once he answers "yes" or "no" as to having an opinion, then he is asked what that opinion is. Capote does an excellent job of describing the consequences of the M'Naghten Rule and of illuminating the clash between legal and medical definitions of insanity:

> "I think that within the usual definitions Mr. Hickock did know right from wrong."
>
> Confined as he was by the M'Naghten Rule ("the usual definitions"), a formula quite color-blind to any gradations between black and white, Dr. Jones was impotent to answer otherwise. But of course the response was a letdown for Hickock's attorney, who hopelessly asked, "Can you qualify that answer?"
>
> It was hopeless because though Dr. Jones agreed to elaborate, the prosecution was entitled to object—and did, citing the fact that Kansas law allowed nothing more than a yes or no answer to the pertinent question. (Capote 330)

The objection is properly sustained under the law. "Much of Part IV dramatizes the premise that conventional morality and criminal law are inadequate means of judging the acts of a Perry Smith" (Pizer "Documentary" 117). Capote, however, goes outside the law to include what the doctor would have said had he been allowed to testify. For the reader this is the kind of inside information that we often crave at an actual trial but are privy to rarely. The doctor would have said that Dick shows characteristics of a severe character disorder and would have recommended that tests be done to rule out the possibility of organic brain damage resulting from his car accident (Capote 331).

The doctor's testimony—or lack thereof—ends Harrison Smith's defense case, and Fleming takes over on behalf of Perry. Three men testify as character witnesses. Joe James, a Native American with whom Perry had lived for two years when he was younger, testifies, " 'Perry was a likeable kid, well liked around the neighborhood—he never done one thing out of the way to my knowledge.' " Don Cullivan, who is an acquaintance from Perry's Army days who was contacted by Fleming to act as a character witness after not having seen Perry in nine years, is described as a "staid young Catholic, a successful engineer who had taken his degree at Harvard, a husband and the father of three children." Cullivan testifies, " 'During the time I knew him in the Army, Perry was a very likeable fellow' " (Capote 324, 332). The prosecution objects to any further general testimony about Perry's character from both witnesses as " 'incompetent, irrelevant, immaterial' " (Capote 332). Reverend Post, the Protestant chaplain from Kansas State Penitentiary, chooses instead to tell the story of Perry's gift to him of a portrait of Jesus Christ that now hangs on his office wall. The Reverend just happens to have photographs of that portrait with him, but Logan Green successfully objects to their admission into evidence. Capote's selection of the testimony of these witnesses suits his plan to humanize the defendants in the reader's eyes and to portray the system as dehumanizing. The more personal details these witnesses can share about the defendants, the more the jury may come to see Perry and Dick as individuals and the more difficult it may be for those jurors to sentence the men to death. The judge rules this evidence is irrelevant.

Finally, Dr. Jones testifies concerning his opinion on Perry's ability to know the difference between right and wrong. This time he has no opinion. Fleming says, " 'You may state to the jury why you have no opinion,' " but Green objects. " 'The man has no opinion, and that's *it*.' " Capote adds, "Which it was, legally speaking" (333). But that finality is overcome by Capote once again providing the reader with what the doctor would have said. The doctor, after consulting with a specialist in forensic psychiatry at the Menninger Clinic, concludes that Perry killed Mr. Clutter "under a mental eclipse, deep inside a schizophrenic darkness." Perry had " 'suddenly discovered' " himself destroying " 'a key figure in some past traumatic configuration.' " Capote points out that Perry had come to the same conclusion himself. He had told Don Cullivan, " 'They [the Clutters] never hurt me. Like other people. Like people have all my life. Maybe it's just that the Clutters were the ones who had to pay for it' " (Capote 338–39).

The defense rests and the closing arguments are about to begin. Once again Capote observes the audience. The "aristocracy" of Finney County are there to hear the closing argument of Logan Green and the instructions of Judge Tate, "esteemed members of their own order" (Capote 339). Lawyers from out of town have also arrived to watch Green perform. The order of presentation is the judge's instructions on the law to the jury and then closing arguments by West, Fleming, Harrison Smith, and Green, in that order. We do not hear the judge's "level-headed" instructions. West's speech reinforces the principle of the Felony-Murder Rule: " 'Can there be a single doubt in your minds regarding the guilt of these defendants? No! Regardless of who pulled the trigger on Richard Eugene Hickock's shotgun, both men are equally guilty.' " West also calls for the death penalty " 'not in vengeance, but in all humbleness' " (Capote 340). Fleming's speech, "described by one journalist as 'soft-shell,' amounted to a mild churchly sermon" (Capote 340). Presumably this journalist is Capote managing to inject his opinion into a "factual" account. The portion of Fleming's speech that Capote shares with us emphasizes that the body should not be destroyed because it is a temple in which the soul resides. "Harrison Smith, although he too appealed to the jurors' presumed Christianity, took as his main theme the evils of capital punishment . . ."   Smith calls the death penalty " 'a relic of human barbarism.' "   " 'All we ask is mercy. Surely life imprisonment is small mercy to ask . . . .' " (Capote 340).   Capote tells us that not everyone was paying attention, but "Green woke them up" (340).   Capote devotes the most space to Green's closing argument and tells us Green works without notes, an impressive feat. Green may perform without notes, but not without some tricks. He tells the jurors that he expected the defense attorneys to use the Bible in their arguments, " 'But *I* can read, too.' " He produces a Bible and begins to read verses:

> Green fumbled, and seemed to accidentally shut the Bible, whereupon the visiting legal dignitaries grinned and nudged each other, for this was a venerable courtroom ploy—the lawyer who while reading from the Scriptures pretends to lose his place, and then remarks, as Green now did, "Never mind. I think I can quote from memory. Genesis Nine, Verse Six: 'Whoso sheddeth man's blood, by man shall his blood be shed.' " (Capote 341)

But, Capote tells us, Green does not want to argue the Bible:

> "Our state provides that the punishment for murder in the first degree shall be imprisonment for life or death by hanging. That is the law. You, gentlemen, are here to enforce it. And if ever there was a case in which the maximum penalty was justified, this is it." (341)

Green reminds the jurors that the motive was money: " 'For forty dollars' worth of loot!' "   Green believes giving the minimum punishment is unthinkable. He ends,

"The next time they go slaughtering it may be *your* family. I say to you,"
he solemnly said, staring at the panel in a manner that encompassed and
challenged them all, "some of our enormous crimes only happen because
once upon a time a pack of chicken-hearted jurors refused to do their duty.
Now, gentlemen, I leave it to you and your consciences." (Capote 342)

When only forty minutes later the jurors return a verdict of guilty and
recommend the death penalty, Dick says to Perry, " 'No chicken-
hearted jurors they!' " Their laughter is captured in a photograph
published in a Kansas paper with the caption " 'The Last Laugh?' "
(Capote 344).

When the jury filed out of the courtroom not one of them would look
at me. I looked each one in the face and I kept thinking, Look at me, look
at me, look at me!
But none of them would. (Hickock 83)

The appeals process in the case takes five years and includes five
stays of execution and three reviews by the U.S. Supreme Court
(Capote 355, 369, 376–77). At one point Dick contacts the Chairman
of the Legal Aid Committee of the Kansas Bar Association, who
appoints an attorney to investigate Dick's claims that a change of
venue should have been granted, that some jurors had indicated a
presumption of guilt and others had known the victims, and that the
defense attorneys were incompetent and inadequate and had not
prepared a defense. The investigating attorney files a habeas corpus
petition to bring these issues before the court. *Habeas corpus* is Latin
for "you have the body," and the term stands for a variety of writs,
the most common of which has for its purpose "to test the legality of
the detention or imprisonment; not whether he is guilty or innocent"
(Nolan and Nolan-Haley 709). A hearing on the habeas corpus
petition is ordered, and the lawyers return to court, this time to defend
themselves. After a hearing that lasts longer than the original trial,
Judge Thiele's ruling is that the defendants had received "a constitu-

tionally fair trial" (Capote 365–69). In a different appeal heard later, the opinion of a three-judge federal Court of Appeals panel supports the ruling of the judge in the habeas corpus action:

> "The attorneys were faced with a situation where outrageous crimes committed on innocent persons had been admitted. Under these circumstances, they would have been justified in advising that petitioners enter pleas of guilty and throw themselves on the mercy of the court. Their only hope was through some turn of fate the lives of these misguided individuals might be spared." (Capote 369)

Capote includes in the text a perceptive discussion of the right of appeal in our system. He says "even an attorney of moderate talent can postpone doomsday year after year." He compares the process to a game of chance "first in the state courts, then through the Federal courts until the ultimate tribunal is reached—the United States Supreme Court. But even defeat there does not signify if petitioner's counsel can discover or invent new grounds for appeal . . ." Capote describes this as "a slow cruel contest" (Capote 370). Would those convicted agree? Some, like Gary Gilmore in *The Executioner's Song*, might. Surely the families of the victims would concur in Capote's sentiment that the process is "a slow cruel contest" during which they are forced to relive the deaths of their loved ones.

Gerald Clarke observes that Perry and Dick were concerned about the narrative Capote was writing for two reasons. First, because their appeals were based on the premise that they had not planned the murders, they did not want Capote to reveal otherwise. Second, they did not want to be memorialized as psychotic killers. Capote never told them that he had completed all of *In Cold Blood* except for the description of the executions (Clarke 346). At the end of their appeals odyssey, Dick and Perry wanted Capote to try to get them another stay. They also wanted him to spend the last day with them before they were hanged on April 14, 1965 (Clarke 353). Capote did not have the heart; he has called the executions " 'the most emotional experience of my creative life' " (qtd. in Grobel 117). Garrett says that Capote " '[wrote] around' " the hangings, and he is right (Garrett 10). By now Capote had become friends with the prisoners. He spent the two days before the executions vomiting in his motel room and arrived at the prison shortly before the executions (Reed 103; Clarke 355). He was the last person to speak to the men. He said they told him good-bye and Perry said, " 'Good-bye. I love you and I always have' " (Grobel 117). Capote accompanied the men to the gallows and cried uncontrollably when it was over (Reed 103). Capote paid for headstones for their graves (Clarke 355).

In an essay in *The Observer* on March 13, 1966, Kenneth Tynan charged that Capote could have done more to save the lives of Smith and Hickock and that he had a moral obligation toward his subjects to do so. Tynan believed, based on his own discussions with legal and psychiatric professionals, that Capote should have hired a psychiatrist to examine and confirm the prisoners' insanity and thereby save their lives. Tynan also alleged that Capote had an interest in the deaths of Smith and Hickock because a reprieve would have altered the text and because Capote could not release the narrative until these men were executed (Tynan 441–46). Capote defended himself in *The Observer* and accused Tynan of many inaccuracies in his essay. As to the contention that Capote could not have released the book until after the executions, he pointed out that he had legal releases from Smith and Hickock and could have published when he chose.

> The sole deterrent was that no one could judge with any certainty whether my book would help or hinder the case as it was being appealed through the Federal courts, and I was not willing to risk publishing anything that might have proved detrimental to Smith and Hickock's chances for a reversal . . . . ("Guts" 449)

Capote notes that "there are only *two* psychiatrists who know at firsthand anything about [the case] whatever" ("Guts" 449).

> No one, not Dr. Jones, nor Dr. Satten, or any of the numerous lawyers
> who worked on the case . . . *ever* thought that a successful appeal could be
> made in Kansas courts (which abide by the McNaghten Rule) on the basis
> of insanity or 'diminished responsibility'. ("Guts" 450)

While Tynan faults Capote for failing to say he did not want these
men to die, in this situation it might be argued that actions speak
louder than words. Capote did not publish during the lives of the
characters and did maintain a relationship with them up until their
deaths. His five year involvement would seem to indicate at least
neutral if not good intentions rather than the grasping, selfish motives
Tynan imputed.

McAleer points out that critics might say that the Clutter murders
were good for Capote's American Dream because he made millions
on the project (580). While McAleer might be right about some of
the critics, Garrett presents a fairer assessment of the reason for the
success of the text: "*In Cold Blood is* classic in the sense that it is an
addition to the ancient and immemorial *genre* of the tale of crime and
punishment which has fascinated writers and readers for as long as
there have been any" (Garrett 4). Capote is certainly working in the
tradition of Dreiser. McAleer lists twenty-one parallels between Perry
and Clyde as well as noting many other similarities between the texts
(581–82). But there is a difference between the two works:

> . . . *In Cold Blood* exemplifies the seemingly random, meaningless crime
> that became symptomatic of America in the sixties. For implicit in the
> story of the Kansas killings are larger questions about the social dislocations
> of the sixties and the failure of conventional morality to explain away the
> senseless violence we read about daily in the newspaper. (Hollowell 85)

The social framework of Dreiser's America was changing, but the
outline of what was acceptable behavior was still visible and acqui-
esced to by a majority of the members of society. In Capote's
America, the traditional markers of family, love, and hard work are

fading. Under the circumstances, an anything-goes attitude on the part of the criminal and a more desperate search for motives by the rest of us prevail. And the legal system does not allow for the thorough discussion of the psychology of the defendants that we seek. Everyone involved in the Clutter case seems to agree that Perry and Dick suffer from some mental disturbance, but the type of mental disturbance does not fall within the legal definition of "insanity" and, therefore, cannot be explored in court. Are we not back to Dreiser's argument that the legal system is ill-equipped to decide certain types of cases?

Hollowell wrote his description of the "social dislocation," "failure of conventional morality," and "senseless violence" of the sixties in 1977, the year Gary Gilmore was executed and two years before the publication of Mailer's *The Executioner's Song*, also a description of a particular crime and a particular time in our history. Mailer's depiction of a crime committed fifteen years after the Clutter killings presents an even bleaker portrait of the inability of the system to deal with someone who has spent almost half his life in prison and does not "fit" in society. In Mailer's world there is no such thing as rehabilitation, no matter how well intentioned our efforts.

NOTES

1. In his *Conversations with Capote*, Lawrence Grobel writes:

> Capote never claimed—as many critics thought he did—that he invented
> narrative journalism or, as *In Cold Blood* came to be labeled, the nonfiction
> novel. He *did* consider it to be a serious new literary form and he did feel
> he had made a major contribution toward its establishment. And he also
> staked the claim to have undertaken the most comprehensive and far-
> reaching experiment in the medium of reportage. (109)

The fact remains that in his *New York Times Book Review* interview
Capote labels *In Cold Blood* a "nonfiction novel" and states, " 'It
seemed to me that journalism, reportage, could be forced to yield a
serious new art form: *the "nonfiction novel," as I thought of it'* "
(emphasis added, qtd. in Plimpton 2). One might be excused for
mistaking this statement for a claim of creation.

2. Tompkins lists the following as West's contribution to the prosecution of the case:

> . . . he was involved in the investigation . . . held daily press conferences
> . . . prepared the brief and the trial outline for the case . . . asked the
> County Commissioners for permission to hire an assistant—Logan Green
> . . . handled much of the examination of the witnesses . . . gave a forty-
> five-minute closing argument . . . represented the County and the State in
> the appeal before the Supreme Court of Kansas. (Tompkins 170)

Tompkins is right; these activities do constitute a "significant" role.

IV

Norman Mailer's *The Executioner's Song*

With Norman Mailer's narrative, published in 1979, we have covered
fifty-four years since *An American Tragedy*, and we will see that
Mailer is still developing the basic themes of Dreiser's work as they
apply to a changed social scene. As Capote's text addresses issues of
the fifties and early sixties, Mailer examines the next decade, up to
Gilmore's execution in 1977. Gary Gilmore's trial reverberates with
familiar procedures and themes, but there are also new social issues
raised. " 'I thought it might be very nice for once just to write a book
which doesn't have answers, but poses delicate questions with a great
deal of evidence and a great deal of material and let people argue over
it' " (Mailer qtd. in Buckley and Greenfield 243), or, as Hayne
describes this technique, "the Maileresque exploration of, and perverse
sympathy with, the psychotic criminal mind . . ." (Hayne 184).

The term "true life novel" on the dust jacket of *The Executioner's
Song* announces the genre of the work we are about to read. Whether
Mailer or his publisher chose this term is unclear, although Mailer said
in a seminar at Yale that he agreed with the publisher's blurb (Fishkin
208 note 13). In the same seminar, Mailer discussed how he saw the
form of the text as supportive of its themes. " 'The tension between
the journalistic aspects of the book and the novelistic aspects of the
book I thought were (sic) ideal for getting at a certain twentieth-
century mood. Always, as one's reading that book, one's saying, how

real is it? Is he telling the truth?' " (qtd. in Fishkin 209). We are back to Meyer Levin's assertion that certain crimes represent the age in which they occur. Mailer is attempting to capture the spirit of the 1970s as he describes the crime and its punishment.

Truman Capote, in an interview with Lawrence Grobel published in 1985, said he had no respect for *The Executioner's Song*. He called it a "nonbook" and said Mailer " ' . . . didn't live through it day by day . . . he never even *met* Gary Gilmore, he didn't do an ounce of research on the book—two other people did all of the research. He was just a rewrite man like you have over at the *Daily News*' " (qtd. in Grobel 113). Mailer did do some of his own interviews, but Capote is correct that Mailer began the project with existing material, and he did have researchers assisting him. Capote claimed that while he was in the middle of writing *In Cold Blood* Mailer had accused him of having a "failure of imagination" (Grobel 113). Capote would later be credited with calling Mailer a "copycat" and criticizing him for his failure to acknowledge Capote's influence on *The Execution-er's Song* (Grobel 113–14). Mailer responded, " 'Well, I just thought that book was so famous that you didn't have to give credit to it' " (qtd. in Grobel 116). In fact, Mailer does credit Capote, in a way, in a 1980 interview: " 'Obviously, I'll be the first to state that if he hadn't done *In Cold Blood*, it's possible that I wouldn't have thought of doing *The Executioner's Song* this way. . . . It's also perfectly possible . . . I might have gone the same route in any case' " (qtd. in Aldridge 270).

The Executioner's Song does demonstrate the influence of Capote's work in more than just its subject matter. Mailer employs a structure similar to, but more complex than, that of *In Cold Blood*. Where Capote alternates two plotlines, Mailer intertwines many. While Capote's text is divided into four parts with scenes within the parts, Mailer uses two major divisions, Book One ("Western Voices") and Book Two ("Eastern Voices"). On one level these divisions represent the two main groups of characters, the families of Utah and the media representatives who come to cover the crime. Olster sees this, however, not as a regional division but as the "tension between manners and mayhem" (411). To Rollyson these two books "dramatize the dialectical tension between documentary form and narrative invention" (*Lives* 295). Each book is divided into seven titled parts and the parts further broken down into titled chapters and then numbered sections. Mailer uses the structural device of double-spacing between groupings of paragraphs within the numbered sections:

> Mailer divides each chapter into short blocks of text, each made up of one or several paragraphs and each usually containing information from one interviewee. In each of these blocks of text, the narrative voice is so subdued and nondescript that the point of view, style of speech, and vocabulary of the interviewee easily dominate it. Each block in effect becomes a vehicle of presentation for a given interviewee . . . . Sometimes a single interviewee's point of view will dominate through a long series of blocks. . . . Other times consecutive blocks will present different interviewees' points of view in order to show how a certain event was seen by each of several eyewitnesses. (McLaughlin 226–27)

Carl Rollyson has an interesting view of the breaks between paragraphs:

> Reality is defined by these frequent intervals of silence, periods of stillness that remind us of how much is left unsaid, of how many characters fail to connect with each other, and of how Gilmore is the most solitary character of all, cut off in large part from humanity and therefore able to murder. ("Biography" 32)

The result of the double-spacing is a "sound bite" feel to the text, which thrusts the thousand-page narrative forward and makes the rapid transitions between characters and locations and time periods and sources of information less disorienting to the reader. It becomes easy to see why Schleifer says "Gossip and voyeurism carry the text along"

(137). This is the pace of America in the 1970s. The contrast between the pace of Mailer's decade and the pace of Dreiser's era is reflected in the density and movement of their prose. The rapid shifting of Mailer's narrative from character to character and consciousness to consciousness gives the impression that we never really know anyone in the text very well, but, by the end of *An American Tragedy*, we have spent so much time with Clyde's thoughts we feel that we understand him.

The prose style of *The Executioner's Song* is a departure for Mailer, who is known for the complexity of his sentence structure and the intrusive nature of his narrative voice. Here Mailer uses simple sentences and an even tone. Arthur Kretchmer called it a "plains voice," and Mailer told him he had picked it up from his sixth wife, Norris Church, who was from Arkansas (Manso 593–94). Joan Didion says this is an "authentic Western voice," and Garvey agrees this is "the plain speech you hear in the midwest and west" (Manso 607; Garvey 140).

> The sparse, anonymous third person narrative, which Larned Bradford [Mailer's editor] called "straight jailhouse prose," was totally devoid of the Mailer ego or the circuitous, sometimes baroque, mental flights which had become characteristic of his work. (Mills 430)

As several critics note, however, Mailer as narrator is not completely absent from the text, just better hidden than usual. Hersey points out what he calls Mailer's "tag lines," "touches of prose, nearly always final lines in the chapterettes . . . each Mailerism is presented as if *within the point of view of a character*. This is not reporting; it is projection" (emphasis in original, Hersey 17–18). Hersey is right; sometimes what the characters say does seem too fortuitous for Mailer's purposes to be considered "true." "Then Gary started to tee off on Val Conlin for making him wait on the truck. 'I'll wreck the place and a couple of his cars too,' he said. 'I'm going to kick them windows in.' It was like opening a bottle that smelled awful" (Mailer

188). While the prose style is simple, Mailer's selection process was complex and the images were carefully shaped.

Book One "Western Voices" opens with Part One "Gary" where we are guided through chapters that describe Gary Gilmore's first month of freedom from prison. At age 35, Gilmore has already spent thirteen years in prison when he becomes eligible for parole. His cousin Brenda arranges for her father, Vern, Gary's uncle, to sponsor Gary with a job in his shoe repair shop and a room in his house in Provo, Utah. Brenda's husband, Johnny, is skeptical: "Gary wasn't coming into an average community. He would be entering a Mormon stronghold. Things were tough enough for a man just out of prison without having to deal with people who thought drinking coffee and tea was sinful" (Mailer 20–21). After his release from prison in April of 1976, Gary arrives in Provo, and he does have a tough time adjusting to a life outside the structured environment of prison. He is childlike, unable to control his impulses and manage his everyday affairs. Gary leaves his job with Vern, going to work for Spencer McGrath doing odd jobs in his recycling machinery business (Mailer 70–71). A month after his release, Gary meets and moves in with the sexually abused, thrice-divorced, 19-year-old mother of two, Nicole Baker Barrett. In this part of the narrative we learn about Gary's desire for a home and family and "to live like other people" (Mailer 43). We also listen to some of Gary's prison stories as he tells them to family members. Through the retrospective musings of the various characters, we get background information about people such as Brenda and her father Vern.

Part Two "Nicole" tells us, once again in flashbacks, the life story of Nicole Barrett as a child. She is sexually abused by a friend of her father, institutionalized at age 13 after she is caught stealing, and pressured by her father to marry at age 14. Her second husband is a drug dealer who fathers her first child. She next lives with a man who picked her up hitchhiking. He fathers her second child, but he beats her and she leaves before the baby is born. Her marriage to her third husband lasts only two weeks. At 19 she is living with her two young children and sewing in a factory when she meets Gary. In this part we learn that Gary has begun to steal. He also begins to tell Nicole about his childhood.

In Part Three "Gary and Nicole" Gary has a fist fight with a neighbor who complained that Gary was paying too much attention to Gary's adolescent second cousin Annette. Nicole first begs the man to drop the assault charges and then threatens to kill him if he won't. The charges are dropped. Gary's proclivity for young girls is again demonstrated when he and Nicole have sex play with young Rosebeth, a friend of the adolescent Laurel who babysits for Nicole's children. Rosebeth is later seduced by Nicole's second husband Barrett when he stops by for a visit. Gary begins shoplifting and is eventually charged with petty theft, to which he pleads guilty. Gary persuades the judge to accept the word of his parole officer in lieu of bail (Mailer 169–70). Gary is drinking beer regularly and taking the drug Fiorinal for his frequent headaches. By now Nicole is beginning to have her doubts about her relationship with Gary and breaks up with him (Mailer 196).

Part Four is entitled "The Gas Station and the Motel" which are the scenes of the two homicides Gary commits. We are first introduced to Colleen and Max Jensen, a Mormon couple with a young child. The background of their courtship is revealed, and we learn that Max is a law school student who is working at a gas station for the summer. We watch as Max leaves for work. Contemporaneously a distraught Gary visits Nicole's mother, Kathryne, asks for the return of a gun he has left with her, and offers to drive Nicole's 17-year-old sister April to the K-Mart. They pick up a truck Gary has financed and drive to Orem, where Gary tells April he wants to make a phone call. He walks to a nearby gas station, has the attendant, Max Jensen, empty his pockets and relinquish his coin changer, takes him into the bathroom, orders him to lie down, and shoots him twice: " 'This one is for me. . . . This one is for Nicole' " (Mailer 227). Afterwards

Gary and April go to a drive-in theater and then visit Brenda. They leave Brenda's, run out of gas, and eventually end up at the Holiday Inn for the night.

We also meet Debbie Bushnell and her husband Ben who manages the City Center Motel. The morning after the gas station killing, Gary takes April home, goes to work, and later keeps his weekly appointment with his parole officer. That evening he stops at a gas station in Provo to ask an acquaintance if he can borrow money and is turned down. He returns to the station at 9:00 p.m., saying his truck will not start. Gary then walks to the nearby City Center Motel, enters the lobby, steals the cash drawer, and shoots the manager, Ben Bushnell, in the head. He is seen in the motel office holding the cash drawer and the gun by Peter Arroyo as Arroyo passes by the lobby. When Gary flees, he discards the cash box and, while trying to get rid of the gun in the bushes, accidentally shoots himself in the thumb. Trailing blood, Gary returns to the gas station and gets into the truck. The gas station owner, having heard over the police scanner about an assault and armed robbery at the motel, takes Gary's license number and calls the police (Mailer 256). Gary drives to the house of an acquaintance and asks for clothes and a ride to the airport. The man calls Brenda, who promises to come for Gary but instead notifies the police. Gary tries to escape, but he is stopped and arrested (Mailer 269).

At this point the trial process, which will be reviewed in detail later, begins. Gary is ultimately convicted and sentenced to death. He chooses a firing squad as the mode of death and refuses to pursue any appeals. No one had been executed in the United States since 1967, and in 1972 the U.S. Supreme Court had ruled that the death penalty statutes as drafted and applied were unconstitutional. Gilmore is sentenced under Utah's new statute. His challenge to the Utah authorities to make him the first man executed in the United States in a decade attracts media attention which will follow Gilmore to his grave. At the end of Book One we begin to learn about Gary's mother Bessie and his brothers Frank, Galen, and Mikal.

Book Two "Eastern Voices" delineates the battle among the lawyers trying to save Gary's life against his wishes, the lawyers attempting to carry out the sentence, and the members of the media jockeying for the rights to Gilmore's story. Characters such as lawyer Dennis Boaz, Mormon prison chaplain Cline Campbell, Utah Assistant Attorney General Earl Dorius, reporter Tamera Smith of the *Deseret News*, and producer Lawrence Schiller are introduced. We learn about Gary's life in prison and about the reaction of his mother Bessie and his brother Mikal to Gary's wish to die. Finally we are informed of the aftermath of Gilmore's actions on his victims, his attorneys, his family, and his friends. The narrative is followed by an afterword.

Lawrence Schiller, a "character" in the text, was the producer who originally began recording Gilmore's experience. After Gilmore's execution, Schiller, who had worked with Mailer on a previous project—not always amicably—called Mailer and asked him to read an interview Schiller and writer Barry Farrell had done with Gilmore for *Playboy* magazine. Mailer was interested, Schiller sent more material, and Mailer started a project he believed would take six months. Two-and-a-half years later *The Executioner's Song* was completed (Mills 424–26; Aldridge 267).

Beyond the material already gathered by Schiller, including interviews with Gary and the letters Gary wrote to his girlfriend, Nicole, while he was in prison, Mailer did his own research including hundreds of interviews (Aldridge 268). He visited Utah six or seven times to conduct interviews spending two months in an apartment in Provo, and he went to Oregon two or three times. He spent the night in the house where Gilmore and Nicole had lived, met Gary's uncle Vern and cousin Brenda, and dined with Assistant Attorney General Earl Dorius, who represented the state during the appeals process. Mailer credits his secretary, Judith McNally, for conducting interviews with the lawyers: " '. . . [M]uch of the jurisprudence in the book comes from her research' " (qtd. in Aldridge 268). Mailer conducted the interviews of Schiller and spoke with Nicole and Gary's mother,

Bessie. While a guest at a seminar on "The Journalist as Novelist" at Yale in 1982, Mailer said,

> "The stuff on Gilmore's mother is probably two-thirds fanciful. The stuff on April, the sister of Nicole, is probably three-quarters fanciful . . . I'd say it was ninety-five percent fictional, in fact, with April . . . ." (qtd. in Fishkin 208)

(These revelations may account for why the reader is never sure whether April is drunk or drugged or mentally ill. She doesn't "act right," but she also doesn't follow any recognizable pattern of acting "wrong.") Schiller explained that collateral research on the project included reviewing newspaper microfilms and television tapes. Mailer also saw the federal prison at Marion, Illinois, where Gilmore had previously been incarcerated. Manso explains that much of Mailer's prison research had to be cut because of the length of the text, published at 1019 pages (Schiller in Manso 584–86; Mills 426). Mailer, perhaps having learned from Truman Capote's experience, included an afterword in *The Executioner's Song* in which he describes the process he used to create the text. According to Mailer editing was done on a variety of sources for several reasons, such as on newspaper stories ". . . to avoid repetition or eliminate confusing references"; on Gary's transcribed interviews ". . . to treat him decently. . . . Transition from voice to print demands no less"; and on Gary's letters, where ". . . it seemed fair to show him at a level higher than his average. . . . His good letters are virtually intact" (Mailer 1021). Mailer does admit that ". . . the story is as accurate as one can make it. This does not mean it has come a great deal closer to the truth than the recollections of the witnesses" (Mailer 1020). The same statement could apply to the depiction of any courtroom proceeding.

On a thematic level, Gary is the outsider who strives to be a part of the American Dream, beginning with a relationship with his new love, Nicole. He views Nicole's leaving as the end of his dream and acts irrationally and violently, as he has often acted in the past. He kills to ease his pain and becomes enmeshed in the Mormon-dominated power structure of Utah. He is sentenced to death, but he manages to wrest some control from the state by refusing to appeal his sentence and demanding his execution as soon as possible. Mailer overlays the basic thematic pattern with themes of psychology, sexuality, religion, and the media.

The issue of Gary's mental state is explored in depth because the defense attorneys hope to use his condition in mitigation of the death penalty. Gary says he feels bad about what he's done, but even he cannot explain why he shot these men. As Mailer sees it:

> "You know we've been sitting smugly on Freud and Jung for 70 years but we don't know a damn thing about human nature, and Gilmore poses questions that psychologists and psychiatrists can't answer, and that's why I'm fascinated by [Gilmore] and that's why I think he's worth the attention." (qtd. in Bragg 254)

We know almost more than we care to about the sexual preferences of the main characters, and the sex acts are described in explicit detail. Very early in the text we are told that Gary prefers young women. "The girls he liked best, he said, were around twenty. It occurred to Vern that Gary wasn't much older when he said good-bye to the world for thirteen years" (Mailer 37). Nicole's version of her first experience with Gary, which occurs within hours of meeting him, is that he couldn't get an erection but wanted to keep trying. "It became straight hard work and it made her mad" (Mailer 89). Because Gary loves to see her naked, Nicole takes off her clothes late one night on the back steps of the First Mormon Church in Provo Park "practically the center of town" (Mailer 97). We know that they shave Nicole's pubic hair in effect returning her to a child-like state (Mailer 142). The fantasies of other male characters are fulfilled when Barrett, Nicole's ex-husband, seduces Rosebeth and when Nicole sees Joe Bob Sears, one of her lovers, with "a calf sucking on her new man" (Mailer 123). The women are not without their desires. April, Nicole's younger sister, removes her halter top to bare her breasts when Gary's parole officer pays a visit to Nicole, and for a time April dates Nicole's first husband (Mailer 136, 172). Nicole has sex with Barrett while living with Gary. In fact she compares notes with Rosebeth who "knew now, she told Nicole, why Gary had never been able to put it in. Too big. Nicole and Rosebeth began to have this long laugh waiting for Gary to get home from work" (Mailer 153). The sexuality of the characters often appears frantic, abusive, and devoid of affection. The sexual encounters portrayed in the narrative serve as an ironic contrast to the Mormon community in which these acts occur.

The theme of religion enters the text in two forms. The first form is the Mormon establishment in Utah. ". . . Utah in *The Executioner's Song* both *suggests* the theocratic principles upon which the nation was founded and *serves*, quite literally, as an illustration of those principles in action" (Olster 410). To Mailer, " 'Mormons epitomize society. . .with a great emphasis on cleanliness, order, discipline . . . the Mormons would have been [Gilmore's] new jailers' " (qtd. in Buckley and Greenfield 237). The second form of religion in the text is Gary's belief in karma and reincarnation. Larry Schiller says Gilmore did discuss reincarnation in his 600–700 pages of letters, and Mailer "didn't go out of his way to highlight Gilmore's stuff about karma" (Manso 386). Mailer discussed reincarnation in an interview:

"Before I wrote a thing about him I felt here's a perfect example of what I've been talking about all my life—we have profound choices to make in life, and one of them may be the deep and terrible choice most of us avoid between dying now and 'saving one's soul'—or at the least, safeguarding one's soul—in order, conceivably, to be reincarnated. Maybe there is such a thing as living out a life too long, and having the soul expire before the body. And here's Gilmore with his profound belief in karma, wishing to die, declaring he wants to save his soul. I thought, here, finally, is the perfect character for me." (qtd. in Aldridge 263)

The media theme is defined by McLaughlin when he asks, "Who creates the news, and how close is it to reality?" (233). McLaughlin views the newspaper and television reporters as people who both "shape" the news by the stories they select and "change" the news when they become part of the story, as they do in the Gilmore case (233). Larry Schiller, whom John Hersey accuses of "commercial sadism," is of course the prime example of the involved media representative, but the cast of minor characters includes Bill Moyers, David Susskind, and Geraldo Rivera (Hersey 14). Mailer is raising important issues about the effect of media attention on the judicial process. The lawyers help subvert prison rules by taping interviews with the prisoner; the newspapers file motions for access to interview the prisoner; and Schiller controls who finds out what about Gilmore. And, as McLaughlin points out, Schiller has an economic interest in how Gilmore's story is presented. Because he needs to create sympathy for Gary, he releases certain stories to the local press (234). It is true that Schiller has an economic interest; it is chilling to think that the money is his sole concern. John Hersey says Mailer devotes space to sex and violence and "skimps the intricate, fascinating, and socially consequential questions of law and philosophy that hovered over the first execution in the country in many years" (21). Mailer does not avoid these issues. The many legal and philosophical questions are there for the reader's consideration as presented through the eyes of those involved directly in the issues. Mailer simply refuses to propose answers to the insoluble.

Part Six in Book One is entitled "The Trial of Gary M. Gilmore," but the trial process, beginning with Gary's arrest and ending with his sentencing, covers 178 pages or seventeen per cent of the text, beginning earlier than Part Six (Mailer 268–446). The appeals process, from a state court appeal to the execution, comprises an even greater portion of the narrative: 463 pages or forty-five per cent (Mailer 481–944). Friedland's observation that in works such as *An American Tragedy* and *Native Son* "the story does not end with the verdict, but continues through the quest for commutation—often a more dramatic process than the investigation and trial themselves" certainly applies equally to Mailer's work (Friedland xxi). As with our three previous texts, however, we will be focusing on the trial process; the appeals process will be presented in summary form.

Gary is read his Miranda rights on arrest. A person taken into custody must be warned:

1. That he has a right to remain silent;
2. that any statement he does make may be used as evidence against him;
3. that he has a right to the presence of an attorney;
4. that if he cannot afford an attorney, one will be appointed for him prior to any questioning if he so desires. (Nolan and Nolan-Haley 998)

After the Bushnell killing on the way to the hospital to have the gunshot wound to his thumb treated, Gary tells Lt. Gerald Nielsen that he wants to "tell [him] about it" (Mailer 275). Nielsen informs Gary that the police want to do a paraffin test on him to detect the presence of any gunpowder on his hands. Gary asks for a lawyer and if he has a right to refuse the test. Nielsen says he does have that right, but the police have the right to do the test by force. Gary consents (Mailer 275). Mailer includes Gary's first interview with Lt. Nielsen in transcript form. Noall Wootton, the Utah County prosecutor, decides to charge Gary with first degree murder for the killing of Ben Bushnell at the motel based on the positive paraffin test and the eyewitness, Peter Arroyo (Mailer 276–81). The Clerk of the City Court of Provo calls Mike Esplin to notify him that he has been appointed Gary's attorney and to ask him to attend the arraignment that same morning. All we know about the arraignment is that the charges are read, and Esplin meets Gary for the first time in the courtroom, speaking to him privately afterwards. Mailer is pointing out here that this is not a very auspicious beginning to an effective attorney-client relationship. Since defendants in first degree murder cases in Utah are permitted two attorneys, Esplin calls Craig Snyder, who agrees to take the case. Esplin tells Gary about Snyder and also that Gary will be charged with the Jensen gas station murder (Mailer 284–85).

Lt. Nielsen's next conversation with Gary is presented in narrative form so that the reader can follow the detective's thought process as he questions Gary. Although Gary has indicated a willingness to meet with the lieutenant, Nielsen has concerns about the fact that he is questioning Gary without his attorney present which could result in an illegally obtained, and therefore inadmissible, confession.

> What would be good about a confession, even if they couldn't use it [in court], was that it would produce information they could then employ to dig up further evidence against the guy. . . . (Mailer 291)

Nielsen gets his confession from Gary. The next day Gary is moved from Provo to Orem to be arraigned for the murder of Max Jensen. After the arraignment, Gary tells his lawyers that he committed both murders and has told Nielsen so, not good news for the defense team (Mailer 296–98). The attorneys are confident the confession cannot be used in court because Gary had not been Mirandized at the jail, only when he was arrested, but they are concerned none the less.

The preliminary hearing in Provo on the Bushnell case, the one for which Gary will go to trial, is a chance for the defense to request a delay and for Wootton to press to go forward. This tactic of forcing the defense to trial as soon as possible came up in Dreiser and Wright as a political issue; here Wootton reveals the practical value of a speedy trial: "He had a lot of witnesses so his problem was to keep the case intact" (Mailer 303). The reader learns later in the narrative about the witnesses who testified at the preliminary hearing (Mailer 374, 377). Nielsen testifies as to Gary's confession, over defense counsel's objection, and the judge comments, " 'If I was sitting as a trial judge, I'd exclude it . . . but for the purposes of a Preliminary Hearing, I'm going to admit it' " (Mailer 374). Peter Arroyo, the eyewitness, testifies for the prosecution, as does Brenda, Gary's cousin:

> On the stand, Brenda told of the phone call Gary made from the Orem
> Police Station. "I asked him what he would like me to tell his mother,"
> Brenda had said on the stand. "He said, 'I guess you can tell her it's
> true.'" Mike Esplin tried to get Brenda to agree Gary meant it was true
> he had been charged with murder. Brenda repeated her testimony, and took
> no sides. Gary found that hard to forgive. (Mailer 377)

Gilmore does not testify (Mailer 374, 303). (Defendants often do not
testify at preliminary hearings because they risk being cross-examined
at trial on the statements they make on the record at the preliminary
hearing.) At the hearing Wootton converses with Gary for the first
time, Gary telling the prosecutor how fair and efficient he is.
Wootton is impressed because "Not every con knew enough to run
that line" (Mailer 303). Gary asks what will happen, and Wootton
says they might execute him. Gary's attorney Craig Snyder approaches Wootton with a plea bargain: Gary pleads guilty to the charge of
first degree murder in exchange for a life sentence rather than the
death penalty. "No way," Wootton responds (Mailer 304). We learn
later that Wootton sees Gary as a "risk to society," and this reasonable
conclusion may be why Wootton is unwilling to bargain over Gary's
life (Mailer 411).

While in jail, Gary makes periodic trips to the mental hospital to
undergo psychiatric evaluation by Dr. John Woods (Mailer 330–33).
He also discusses his situation with a fellow prisoner, Gibbs, who
advises Gary that a good lawyer could get him second degree and he
could be paroled in six years. " 'I can't afford a good lawyer . . . .
The state pays for my lawyers. . . . My lawyers work for the same
people that are going to sentence me' " (Mailer 355–56). Gary is
right, Esplin and Snyder are paid by the state, and this fact will
become a constant refrain on Gary's journey through the legal system.
When Gary tells Gibbs that Dr. Woods is going to pronounce him
sane and competent to stand trial, Gary adds, " 'What do you expect?

He's paid by the same people who pay my lawyers. The State of Utah. I can't win for losing' " (Mailer 368–69).

Defense attorney Mike Esplin was in private practice before becoming a Public Defender in Provo the previous year (Mailer 376). Gary Snyder is in private practice, hired by the state to assist in Gary's representation. Mailer goes into great detail concerning the strategy of the defense attorneys. He also educates the reader on the legal process:

> A trial for murder in Utah was conducted in two parts. If the defendant was found Guilty in the First Degree, a Mitigation Hearing had to be held right after. One could then introduce witnesses who were there to testify to the character of the accused, good or bad. After such testimony, the Jury would go out a second time, and decide between life imprisonment and death. (Mailer 375)

(We saw the same mitigation procedure followed when Bigger entered a guilty plea in *Native Son*.) As in the works by Dreiser, Wright, and Capote, defense attorneys Esplin and Snyder are as concerned with their position in the community as they are with an effective defense. Local lawyers gather in the Provo Courthouse coffee shop, "and a young lawyer could do service or injury to his reputation among colleagues" when defending a first degree murder case, not the usual fare in Provo (Mailer 373). Esplin and Snyder are especially aware of the impact of their client's confession, which will not be admitted as evidence at trial but is now common knowledge:

> Much of the promise was out of the defense. A lawyer without a reputation for probity might be able to ignore the fact that half the legal community of Provo now knew, after the Preliminary Hearing, that Gilmore had confessed, and the other half, via the coffee shop, would soon find out. That was bound to inhibit any really imaginative defense. It would not be comfortable before the fact of such a confession to work up the possibility that Bushnell's death was an accident in the course of a robbery. (Mailer 374–75)

Esplin and Snyder admit the accident defense is still possible even allowing for the fact that the absence of powder burns on the victim proves that the gun was held to his head during the shooting. Since the weapon, a Browning .22 Automatic, has one of the most sensitive triggers, the attorneys could still argue that the gun went off accidentally while Gary was trying to frighten the victim. The gun *did* go off accidentally when Gary was throwing it away in the bushes and shot himself in the hand (Mailer 375).

> Yet, that argument could now be employed only as one of several possibilities during a general summation to the Jury. You could not build your case on it, not when many a lawyer in Provo, given the existence of the confession, would see such tactics as sleazy. (Mailer 375)

The defense attorneys know that the absence of powder burns is the strongest evidence against Gary, and, combined with the shell casing found next to the victim's body, the trail of blood from the gun to the gas station, and Peter Arroyo's eyewitness testimony, the case is very solid (Mailer 374). The attorneys review the potential witnesses for the defense who could testify at the mitigation hearing. Gary is uncooperative. He will not allow Nicole to testify. The lawyers talk to Gary's mother, Bessie, but her arthritis is so bad she cannot travel from Oregon. They talk to Spencer McGrath, Gary's boss, but he is not eager to testify on Gary's behalf. They never talk to Gary's uncle Vern—Gary has said his relationship with his relatives is not good—and a state hospital report of an interview with Vern about Gary is not very reassuring (Mailer 377–78). They talk to Brenda, whose testimony at the preliminary hearing was so damaging, and decide she would be a "dangerous" witness (Mailer 377).

> They were down to searching for a psychiatrist who would declare Gilmore insane. Failing that, Snyder and Esplin were looking to find a paragraph in one of the psychiatric reports or even a sentence they could use. (Mailer 378)

Mailer includes the text of three such reports to illustrate the fact that none is useful to the defense (Mailer 378–82). The attorneys consult Dr. John Woods, who has seen Gary at the state mental hospital:

> Woods thought that if Gary's defense was to be based on his mental condition, then Snyder and Esplin had to come up with an argument that would connect the psychotic to the psychopathic. Not easy. The law recognized insanity. You could always save the neck of a psychotic. Psychopathy, however, was more of a madness of the moral reflexes, if you could begin to use such a term (which you couldn't) in a Court of Law.
>
> *****
>
> Of course, Gary did fit into a psychiatric category. There was a medical term for moral insanity, criminality, uncontrolled animality—call it what you will. Psychiatrists called it "psychopathic personality," or, same thing, "sociopathic personality." It meant you were antisocial. In terms of accountability before the law, it was equal to sanity. The law saw a great difference between the psychotic and the psychopathic personality.
>
> *****
>
> The psychopath had fantasies. The psychotic had hallucinations.
>
> Maybe they could attack the problem here. The line between fantasies and hallucinations would certainly not be precise. (Mailer 383–84)

The longer we listen to Dr. Woods speculate, the more hopeless we see Gary's position to be under the law. Here Mailer is highlighting a broader social issue:

> They had to recognize, Woods warned, that the law wanted to keep psychopathy and psychosis apart. If the psychopath were ever to be accepted as legally insane, then crime, judgment, and punishment would be replaced by antisocial act, therapy, and convalescence. (Mailer 384)

Or, put another way, "The psychopath's hunger for immediacy in all things can't help but threaten a culture committed to deferred and displaced satisfactions" (Edmundson 436). Woods does agree to testify for Gary in the mitigation hearing (Mailer 392).

Woods suggests one final psychiatric possibility—a report by a doctor at Oregon State Penitentiary in 1974 that labels Gary as paranoid and "unable to control his hostile and aggressive impulses" (Mailer 396). But Gary objects to that doctor, "[o]f all the dirty, mean, rotten sons of bitches," evaluating him, and the doctor when contacted declines the invitation to testify (Mailer 396). Woods finally recommends to Esplin and Snyder that Gary could use more experienced attorneys. "He said to them as diplomatically as he could, Why don't you get somebody else in on this who can pull some shots? He couldn't get across. They kept on trying to get some evaluation of Gary as a victim of mental illness" (Mailer 397).[1]

Gary includes his view of the defense strategy in a letter to Nicole:

> "All Snyder and Esplin want to do is leave themselves a good case for appeal. That's the way they're paid by the state to think. I'm not saying they are paid to sell me out, I'm not paranoid about it. But they are court appointed lawyers, they don't have the resource to do a proper job. I'll get no more than a token defense from them." (Mailer 401)

This is a perceptive and practical view of his situation. For her part Nicole attempts to convince the best criminal defense attorney in Utah to represent Gary. The lawyer agrees to talk to Gary but never shows up for the arranged meeting (Mailer 399–401).

The prosecutor for Utah County, Noall Wootton, is facing the biggest murder case he has ever tried. He is especially careful to observe the legal technicalities and to avoid any conversation about the case with Gary that might later require Wootton's testimony in court (Mailer 276–77). Wootton believes the best lawyer he ever met was his father, whose firm he joined right out of law school (Mailer 276, 409). Before becoming a prosecutor, Wootton had been a defense attorney, but "the punks wanted to get off at all costs, guilty or not. Noall couldn't buy that" (Mailer 410). Wootton recalls one of the biggest cases he prosecuted; it is reminiscent of Clyde Griffiths's situation in *An American Tragedy*:

. . . Francis Clyde Martin . . . had been forced to get married because his girl was pregnant. Martin took his new wife in the woods and stabbed her twenty times, cut her throat, cut the unborn baby out of her body, stabbed the baby, went home.

*****

In that case Wootton had decided not to go for the death penalty. Martin was a nice-looking eighteen-year-old high-school student with no criminal record. Just a kid in a terrible trap who ran amok. (Mailer 410)

What Wootton sees as different about Gary is that he is a "risk to society" as long as he is alive (Mailer 411). When Wootton approaches a case, he likes to anticipate opposing counsel's strategy (Mailer 426). He also has a technique for dealing with the jury:

. . . Wootton's strategy was to pick one member who was strong and intelligent and one who, in his opinion, wasn't. You tried to present your case in story form to the juror who was not intelligent, whereas you argued the contradictions before the one who was. (Mailer 438)

The day before the trial, the defense attorneys hold a conference with Gary. Gary does not want to fake insanity: " 'I resent having my intelligence insulted' " (Mailer 411). He still refuses to have Nicole testify on his behalf even after she has been subpoenaed by the state, and, because Nicole is now a witness in the case, Gary refuses to allow the attorneys to request that the courtroom be cleared of prosecution witnesses while the state is presenting its case-in-chief:

Gary's lawyers said this had to give Wootton an advantage. His witnesses would be able to hear what the ones before them said. Everything in Wootton's presentation would come out smoother. Didn't matter, Gary told them.

Snyder and Esplin tried to change his mind. When witnesses, they said, were not able to hear each other, they felt more nervous on the stand. Didn't know what they were stepping into. That was a great deal for the defense to give away just so they could have Nicole in the courtroom. (Mailer 412)

Gary is adamant.

Mailer covers jury selection in a single sentence, understandable in a narrative that already runs to over a thousand pages. The trial does not begin auspiciously for the defense. Esplin must ask Judge Bullock to send the jury out of the courtroom so an issue of law can be discussed. (The jury is sent out of the courtroom in instances when the issue being discussed—of fact, law, or procedure—is not proper for the jury to hear.) The judge is not impressed with this "issue of law" when Esplin explains "that the defendant, against their advice, did not wish any of the prosecution witnesses to be excluded. It was a poor start. Many a Judge lost respect for a lawyer who could not show a client his best interest" (Mailer 412). Here Mailer includes a brief excerpt of the exchange of Bullock, Esplin, and Gary from the trial transcript (Mailer 412). He will use this technique throughout the trial, juxtaposing straight prose with the question-and-answer format taken from the transcript.

Wootton's opening statement includes the standard summary of testimony, as well as the rhetorical technique of repetition, in this case the repeated phrase "they will tell you . . . ." " 'Each [witness],' he said, 'will give you a small piece of the overall story' " (Mailer 413). There is no indication that the defense attorneys present an opening statement. Either they chose to reserve their opening statement to present before their case-in-chief or Mailer chose not to describe whatever opening was given. The narrative moves forward to the state's case.

Mailer most often summarizes the testimony, but he sometimes includes material in transcript form. The first witness is a draftsman who drew a plan of the motel. Mailer notes that the defense attempts on cross-examination to "raise doubts on small points" (Mailer 413). The defense attorney gets the draftsman to admit that the drawing does not account for any plants outside the building (Mailer 413). This sketch will be submitted into evidence as the first of eighteen prosecution exhibits (Mailer 414). Next to testify is the detective who took the photographs of the motel office, and he admits on cross that the drapes may have been moved before the photos were taken (Mailer 414). The third witness is the man who saw the victim at the scene and drove the victim's wife to the hospital. The defense knows not to question this witness: "Esplin was not going to intensify the vividness of those scenes by cross-examination" (Mailer 414). The medical examiner who performed the autopsy testifies to the absence of powder burns on the victim, which would indicate that the gun was held next to his head when fired. The best the defense can do on cross is to get the doctor to admit that he did not examine the actual gun in this case, a fact that has no bearing on the doctor's opinion concerning the powder burns (Mailer 414–15). The service station attendant testifies that he saw blood on Gary's hand, and a police officer tells how he found the gun in the bushes and followed a trail of blood to the gas station. The defense is able to elicit the fact that the detective who had the cartridge case and gun photographed at the scene did not take the photographs himself. "You never knew when a few small gains could contribute to the final effect" (Mailer 415). This same detective testifies that a single fingerprint found on the gun was too smudged for the FBI to identify (Mailer 416). On direct, Wootton does not question Lt. Nielsen about Gary's confession. Nielsen just says that Gary had a gunshot wound of the hand when he was arrested. An FBI agent states that the two cartridges came from the gun found in the bushes (Mailer 416).

Mailer has alerted us earlier in the text that Peter Arroyo, the man who saw Gary with the cash drawer and the gun in the motel lobby, will be the state's star witness. "Arroyo made a perfect appearance. He was a family man who spoke in a clear and definite voice. If you were filming a movie and wanted a witness for the prosecution who could hurt the defense, you would cast Peter Arroyo" (Mailer 374). Mailer is stating a courtroom fact of life: appearances count, as do the witness's voice, attitude, and demeanor. Arroyo's testimony is presented in question-and-answer form for both his direct and cross examinations, presumably because of the importance of what he has to say. Arroyo describes seeing Gary at the motel and says he recalls the look in Gary's eyes: "Not hard to comprehend what Arroyo meant. Gilmore had been glaring at Wootton throughout the testimony" (Mailer 418). The prosecution rests; surprisingly, so does the defense. The judge will instruct the jurors in the morning.

Gary complains about the handling of his defense. He wants to know why a psychiatrist was not called, and the lawyers explain that no one would testify that Gary was legally insane but that a psychiatrist will be called in the mitigation hearing. " 'Couldn't we have called somebody?' he asked, 'just for appearance's sake?' " (Mailer 419). The attorneys review for Gary the favorable evidence that the jury can consider in their deliberations, such as the fact that there was never a test to prove that the trail of blood matched Gary's type, that there were no fingerprints from the gun, that the prosecution never entered the money stolen into evidence, and that the prosecution had not used Gary's confession. "Not easy to sentence a man to death, was their unvoiced remark" (Mailer 420). Gary's dissatisfaction with his lawyers is clear in a letter to Nicole:

> "I had told you that I didn't expect much from Snyder and Esplin but I was not prepared for the fact that they intended to put up absolutely no defense at all. . . . I thought they would at least try to get a second degree conviction. . . . They acted guilty and defensive as a motherfucker when I confronted em about it after the trial. They didn't even try. All they want to do is leave theirself a case for appeal and they haven't even done that. That's the way it is with court appointed lawyers." (Mailer 418–19)

Gary decides he wants to testify, and the attorneys try to discourage him. They do not look forward to asking the judge to reopen the case after they have already rested. They also reconsider and then reject the idea of having Nicole testify on Gary's behalf (Mailer 420).

Once again the defense attorneys face the challenge of asking the judge to clear the court room so they can discuss an unusual issue.

Mailer frequently includes the discussions of the attorneys as they try to do their best for their client and still manage to maintain their professional images. This material emphasizes Mailer's view that, in the end, the outsider and the insiders are equally trapped in the system. Esplin informs the judge that Gary wishes to testify, and the judge questions the defendant. The incident is taken from the transcript:

> THE COURT "What evidence do you have that you want to present?"
> MR. GILMORE "Apparently I don't have any, according to my lawyers."
>   *****
> MR. GILMORE "I feel myself that I have a good insanity defense or at least a basis of it. But apparently the doctors don't concur. But the conditions that I talked to the doctors under were adverse."
>   *****
> THE COURT "My question to you is: Do you want to have the Court reopen the case . . . be sworn as a witness and testify?" (Mailer 424–25)

The judge asks Gary whether he understands that he will be subject to cross-examination, that he will be compelled to answer the questions, and that the questions and answers may be incriminating. Defense attorney Snyder wants one additional statement placed on the record: that the attorneys have consulted four psychiatrists, that those doctors would testify that Gary has a mental disorder known as psychopathic or antisocial behavior, that such a disorder does not constitute the defense of insanity, and that without expert testimony the Court will not even instruct the jury on the insanity defense. This statement of record is necessary to protect the attorneys should Gary later decide to challenge their competence. Gary's response to this recitation of his lawyers' efforts is to withdraw his request to reopen the case. "It was as if a resignation had come over him as he argued, a gloom, and he now saw the case as Snyder and Esplin had seen it weeks before" (Mailer 426). Wootton is especially confused:

He had not really known what he could do to refute it if Gary got on the stand and told a convincing tale.

*****

Only later, did Wootton find out that Gary wouldn't cooperate with his lawyers. At this point, he could hardly understand why they had rested, but decided the reason they didn't put Gilmore on the stand had to be his personality. He must have an explosive temper. (Mailer 427)

Again, Mailer describes this scene in detail in order to support his view that the process has taken on a life of its own and the participants are merely players in the game.

The prosecutor is ready to make his closing argument. Wootton reviews the testimony with emphasis on that of the medical examiner. He reminds the jurors that the gun was placed directly against the victim's head; this was not an accidental shooting. The prosecutor asks the jurors to be fair to Gary but also to " 'judge [the case] fairly from the point of view of Benny Bushnell's widow and his child and the child yet to be born' " (Mailer 427).

Esplin begins the closing argument for the defense with the traditional complimenting of the jury, usually for their careful attention. The defense tries two approaches, first suggesting an alternate scenario to that proposed by the state and then chipping away at the state's evidence. Esplin's alternate scenario is that the perpetrator was caught in the act of taking money by Bushnell, who was then shot. Esplin points out that under those facts the original crime would be theft, not robbery. It is not clear why Esplin makes this distinction between the two crimes. Mailer in an interview gives one opinion:

"He could have probably gotten life imprisonment if he'd wanted it, by saying that he did it for the money and shot these men in the course of committing the crimes, because if you kill someone in the course of an armed robbery, you are much more likely to get life than the death sentence." (qtd. in Buckley and Greenfield 232)

The question of premeditation and intent appears to be the key in

Mailer's analysis. Going to rob and then killing is not the same as going to kill. But why is Esplin arguing a difference between robbery and theft? Rather than the distinction Mailer makes, a more legally sound argument is that during a theft a weapon need not be involved while in a robbery you are armed by definition. Therefore it is a stronger defense argument to say the defendant went to steal without the intent to do violence than to admit the defendant went armed to rob.

Esplin continues his campaign to establish reasonable doubt. He implies that the state could have called the victim's wife, who was in the family living quarters off the lobby, but they did not. The state has not produced the money stolen. The gun accidentally went off in the bushes. No one actually saw the killing; Arroyo saw only the defendant and a gun he could not identify. Esplin also asserts that Gary would have been pretty stupid to have parked at the gas station down the street, where he could easily be identified, if his intention was to kill someone. Esplin ends by reminding the jurors that if they have any reasonable doubts they should either find the defendant guilty of the lesser included offense of second degree criminal homicide or acquit the defendant. Esplin delivers his plea in such an emotional manner that several of the jurors are in tears and colleagues later ask how he could put on such a good act. Esplin acknowledged he was surprised at the level of his genuine emotion (Mailer 428).

The state waives rebuttal argument and the jury retires. Esplin then makes a motion for a mistrial based on the prejudicial quality of the prosecutor's closing remarks about the victim's widow. The motion is denied. The jury returns an hour and twenty minutes later with a verdict of guilty in the first degree. The mitigation hearing will be held that afternoon.

Mailer presents an accurate portrayal of the grapevine process in a courthouse, especially in a closely knit community, when he tells us that during the recess between the guilty verdict and the mitigation hearing a crowd gathered for the afternoon session. "A legal process would decide a man's life—that had to be an awesome afternoon" (Mailer 430). Judge Bullock explains the purpose of the mitigation hearing and alerts the participants that hearsay evidence is allowed during this proceeding. Hearsay is defined as:

> [T]hat species of testimony given by a witness who relates, not what he knows personally, but what others have told him, or what he has heard said by others. . . . Hearsay evidence is testimony in court of a statement made out of the court, the statement being offered as an assertion to show the truth of matters asserted therein, and thus resting for its value upon the credibility of the out-of-court asserter. (Nolan and Nolan-Haley 722)

The defense attorneys must work with what they have under the circumstances:

> Since hearsay could prove injurious to Gary, Craig Snyder (who was doing the Mitigation Hearing even as Mike Esplin had handled the trial) was trying his best to lay grounds for appeal. Snyder objected often, and Judge Bullock overruled him almost as often. Let one ruling by the Judge be declared in error by a higher Court, and Gary could not be executed. So Craig Snyder was counting as much on the strength of future appeal as on his chances of avoiding the death sentence now. (Mailer 430)

The detective who had testified at trial to taking the crime scene photographs now gets back on the stand to testify concerning a telephone call he had made during the recess. He had spoken to the Assistant Superintendent of Oregon State Penitentiary, who told him Gary " 'assaulted someone with a hammer' " and " 'assaulted a dentist' " and as a consequence was moved from Oregon to the federal penitentiary in Marion, Illinois. Snyder objects. A professor of chemistry testifies as to Gary's blood alcohol level at the time of arrest, five hours after the crime. Considering the possible variations in the level over time, the expert states that Gary would have known what he was doing at any of the possible levels. On cross, Snyder gets the witness to concede that Gary's blood alcohol level at the time

of the crime could have been as much as twice the level of intoxication required to convict under the drunk-driving statute and that
Fiorinal taken while drinking would increase the level of intoxication.
The next witness is a representative from the probation and parole
department filling in for Gary's parole officer, who is on vacation.
Snyder objects. Snyder then argues that the next witness, a detective
investigating the murder of Max Jensen, should be prevented from
testifying because his testimony will be "entirely prejudicial" (Mailer
431). The detective testifies Gary has been arrested in that case. The
final witness for the state is Gary's cousin Brenda, who has been
subpoenaed. She repeats her testimony from the preliminary hearing,
that when she told Gary that his mother was going to want to know
if the charges were true, Gary responded " 'Tell her that it's true,' "
but "that she couldn't be certain whether Gary meant it was true that
he committed murder, or true that he was charged with murder"
(Mailer 433). Brenda is unhappy to have to give evidence against
Gary, and she is afraid what Nicole might do to her (Mailer 432–33).
The state rests.

Dr. John Woods testifies on Gary's behalf. Woods says that a
psychopath has the capacity to know the wrongfulness of conduct but
chooses not to know, and that alcohol and Fiorinal "would impair his
judgment and would loosen the controls on a person that already has
very poor control of himself . . ." (Mailer 433). Woods also tells of
a childhood experience Gary related about how he used to race a train
over the trestle to see if he could beat the train off the trestle before
being thrown into the gorge below (Mailer 434). On cross, Wootton
quotes from Woods's own report that says that Gary is not psychotic
or insane, that he was not mentally ill at the time of the crime, and
that Gary's alcohol and drug use had been considered when preparing
the report. Woods admits that his opinion is still the same opinion he
gave in the report from which Wootton is quoting (Mailer 434). The
defense attorneys consider and reject the idea of calling Lt. Nielsen to
testify as to Gary's remorseful statement " 'I really feel bad. . . . I

hope they execute me for it' " (Mailer 434). Nielsen knows too much
damaging information that could come out on cross.

Gary is the final defense witness in mitigation. Mailer presents
this testimony almost entirely in transcript form, and we hear Gary tell
his story in his own words. Gary says he guesses he killed Bushnell,
but he did not go to the motel with the intent to kill. He does not
know why he killed Bushnell. " 'I felt like there was no way what
happened could have been avoided, that there was no other choice or
chance for Mr. Bushnell. It was just something that, you know,
couldn't be stopped' " (Mailer 435). Gary says he felt as though he
had no control, and he uses the simile he has used before in the case,
that it was as though he was watching a movie, watching someone
else act. Gary explains that he told the train trestle incident to the
doctor to try to compare his feeling on the night of the crime to his
racing the train: " 'I sometimes feel I have to do things and seems like
there's no other chance or choice' " (Mailer 436). The defense
attorneys are not convinced they have accomplished their goal of
having Gary appear remorseful. They think Gary was "too calm, too
solemn, even a little remote" (Mailer 436). Gary's demeanor changes,
however, during cross-examination. He becomes hostile, and his
answers to Wootton's questions are curt. " 'How did you kill him?'
Wootton began. 'Shot him,' said Gilmore" (Mailer 436). He says he
does not remember much detail from that night and that he does not
remember taking the cash box or money with him. Gary remains true
to his vow not to involve Nicole in his case; on the stand he refuses
to discuss Nicole at all (Mailer 437–38). Wootton thinks, "No
remorse at all. Not the smartest way to fight for your life" (Mailer
438). Wootton notes that, although the jury had not been looking at
Gary before he testified, they now stared.

After what he considers an effective cross-examination, Wootton
purposely keeps his closing argument short. He again refers to the
victim's widow and children, and Snyder objects once again. This
time the judge reserves his ruling on the motion but requests that

Wootton not include such material in the balance of his argument. Wootton instead cites the failure to rehabilitate Gary, saying Gary has graduated to killing his robbery victims so they cannot testify against him. Gary's history of escape from reform school and prison in Oregon and his history of violence in prison mean " 'He's a danger if he escapes, he's a danger if he doesn't' " (Mailer 439). Wootton ends by arguing that Gary should be executed for what he did to Bushnell and his family.

Snyder's closing is based on more general principles: Gary is a person and has a right to his life. Snyder asserts Gary needs treatment more than execution. When Snyder says Gary is thirty-six years old, Gary interrupts the speech to correct his attorney: he is only thirty-five. In response to the suggestion in Wootton's closing that life in prison does not mean forever, Snyder says Gary would not be eligible for parole, if at all, for a long time. Finally, Snyder reminds the jury that in order to impose the death penalty, their vote must be unanimous: " 'I would ask each of you to search your own conscience and to impose in this case life imprisonment' " (Mailer 440). Esplin declines the judge's offer to make his own remarks to the jury. When Gary is asked if he has anything to say to the jury, he says, " 'Well, I am finally glad to see that the Jury is looking at me. . . . No, I have nothing to say' " (Mailer 441).

The verdict is death, and Gary's choice for the mode of death is the firing squad. The execution date is set.

> Gary looked over calmly, and said, "Wootton, everybody around here looks like they're crazy. Everybody but me." Wootton looked back and thought, "Yes, at this moment, everybody could be crazy, except Gary." (Mailer 442)

Wootton acknowledges to himself that Gilmore is more intelligent and better educated, albeit self-educated, than Wootton is, and Wootton believes the system has failed Gary (Mailer 442).

The night of Gary's sentencing, Gary's brother Mikal tells their mother, " '. . . they haven't executed anybody in the country for ten years, and they aren't about to start with Gary' " (Mailer 446). Not unless Gary decides he wants to die. The appeals process in the case is sent into chaos once Gary refuses to pursue his right of appeal and instead demands to be executed. "Gilmore's deep joke consists in capitulating and becoming just the kind of well-disciplined subject everyone always wanted him to be, but at the wrong moment" (Edmundson 439). Mailer sees " 'an extraordinary manipulation that he could put upon the normal social procedure . . . ' " (qtd. in Buckley and Greenfield 235). Gary's refusal to abide by the rules supports the theme of the outsider who rebels against the power structure. Gary's family and outside groups intervene on his behalf, and the media descend. "[T]he strong smell of money given off by this death-row drama drifted east with the weather systems and attracted New York's media vultures" (Hersey 13).

As mentioned earlier, the portrayal of the appeals process in the narrative is more extensive than the coverage of the trial and deals with the theme of the negative impact of the media on the judicial process. Book Two, "Eastern Voices," highlights the actions of the legal and journalistic communities as they participate in Gary's death-wish and chronicles the journey of Gary's family and friends.

Gary's trial lawyers believe Gary has a good case on appeal. They feel Gary's sentence will be reduced to life in prison on one of three grounds: first, the Utah death penalty statute is "constitutionally defective" because it does not provide for a mandatory review of a sentence of death; second, at the mitigation hearing the judge improperly admitted evidence of Gary's arrest in the Jensen murder; and, third, it was reversible error for the judge to allow the remarks concerning the victim's widow during the state's closing argument at trial (Mailer 481). The attorneys are confident; Gary asks if he can fire them.

Gary goes before Judge Bullock to withdraw his motion for a new trial (Mailer 483). His lawyers, wanting to protect themselves and to protect Gary should he change his mind, file an appeal against his wishes (Mailer 505). Gary is contacted by an off-beat lawyer/writer named Dennis Boaz, who wants to represent him in his right-not-to-appeal case. The ACLU and the NAACP decide to oppose Gary's pursuit of execution (Mailer 507).[2] Boaz goes before the Supreme Court of Utah to have the motion for appeal filed by the trial attorneys set aside and the stay of execution vacated. The Utah Supreme Court vacates the stay and once again the execution can go forward (Mailer 522–24).

One of the jurors has written a letter to the *Provo Herald* asking why, if there was no error in the trial court, has Gilmore's case gone before the U.S. Supreme Court? Judge Bullock, in a highly unusual move, has his clerk notify the jurors that the judge will meet with them unofficially to discuss the case if the jurors are interested. All of the jurors accept the invitation to meet the judge in the courtroom after hours. "People hadn't been executed since 1967, so it was highly appropriate that delays take place. But he wanted the Jury to understand that they had not done their part of the job incorrectly" (Mailer 722). It is not often that a judge will go out of his way to reassure the jurors, but, then, this is not turning out to be a typical case.

Mailer makes extensive use in Book Two of clippings from a variety of publications to keep us updated on the progress toward execution and the activities of the various participants. Several media representatives become intimately involved with Gary's case. One is a young female reporter from the local paper, Tamera Smith, who befriends Nicole and eventually gains access to Gary's letters to her (Mailer 527). Another is Larry Schiller, the producer who ultimately brings the Gilmore project to Norman Mailer, who approaches Gary for the film and publication rights to Gary's life story (Mailer 582). And, of course, a plethora of lawyers are involved, both willingly and unwillingly, representing the Utah Attorney General's office, the

ACLU, the NAACP, and various individuals. At one point Gary writes a letter, published in the *Provo Herald,* asking those who oppose his execution, especially the ACLU and the NAACP, to " 'butt out' " (Mailer 762). Mailer demonstrates that everyone has the opportunity to express his opinion through the press.

While the battle is raging, Nicole smuggles pills to Gary in prison, and she and Gary attempt suicide (Mailer 559). Both survive. Gary returns to prison; Nicole goes to a mental hospital. Gary fires Boaz and hires Bob Moody and Ron Stanger (Mailer 623):

> ". . . they were both Mormons and both well established small-town lawyers. That means they were very dependable, very regular, very decent men more or less—I say more or less because it's hard to think of a lawyer as being *very* decent . . ." (Mailer qtd. in Bragg 255)

Gary goes on a hunger strike. Before the Utah Board of Pardons Gary asserts,

> "I simply accepted the sentence that was given to me. I have accepted sentences all my life. I didn't know I had a choice in the matter.
> "When I did accept it, everybody jumped up and wanted to argue with me. It seems that the people, especially the people of Utah, want the death penalty but they don't want executions and when it became a reality they might have to carry one out, well, they started backing off on it.
> "Well, I took them literal and serious when they sentenced me to death just as if they had sentenced me to ten years or thirty days in the county jail or something. I thought you were supposed to take them serious. I didn't know it was a joke." (Mailer 657)

The legal wars in the state court and the U.S. Supreme Court continue in the form of various motions, writs, and stays. Gary attempts suicide a second time unsuccessfully (Mailer 726). The legal community is involved in Gary's case up to the last moment before he is executed in front of a firing squad on January 17, 1977 (Mailer 957).

The Executioner's Song accomplishes Mailer's goal of " '[posing] delicate questions with a great deal of evidence and [letting] people argue over it' " (qtd. in Buckley and Greenfield 243). This aspect of the narrative has been adversely criticized (Hersey 21; McWilliams 116). "Nonfiction criminal novels [in which McWilliams also includes *In Cold Blood*] offer no solutions for the improving of criminal procedures because they offer no solutions for the causes of criminality" (McWilliams 116). It is true that "Mailer found he could not explain Gilmore." It is also true that Mailer believed "it was 'more interesting not to' " explain his protagonist (Rollyson *Lives* 286). McWilliams is placing an unreasonable burden on the writer if he is suggesting that Mailer must be able to discover the causes of Gilmore's criminal behavior before he embarks on a narrative about Gilmore's crime.

Perhaps one of the people most interested in the sources of Gilmore's crimes is his younger brother Mikal who wrote about his exploration of the family history in his 1994 book *Shot in the Heart*. What he discovered was a legacy of deception and brutality. Frank Jr., the oldest Gilmore brother, says about the severe beatings by their father, "And that's what built up in us, resentment, because even as kids you know you are being overpunished for simple things" (Gilmore 125). Frank also speculates that his father beat the children so their mother Bessie would intervene, thus giving Frank Sr. the excuse to argue with Bessie. Mikal sees these early, unjust punishments as the source of Gary's rebellion against authority throughout his life. One other possible source of the anger that Frank Gilmore Sr. took out especially on Gary may have been Frank Sr.'s suspicion that Gary was not his child but rather the product of an affair between Bessie and Robert Ingram, Frank's grown son by a first marriage. The bitter irony is that Bessie had confided to her sister Ida that Frank Jr., not Gary, was Ingram's son (Gilmore 391–92).

Book Two of Mailer's narrative raises important issues of freedom of the press, the right to die, the death penalty, and the judicial process. Mailer's portrait of those involved in the legal process is probably the least adversely critical of the four writers we have examined. The lawyers in *The Executioner's Song* are admirable in comparison to the media representatives. As Schleifer observes, the book presents ". . . what Dreiser called an American *tragedy* as a media event" (125). The lawyers have the usual self-interest, but the arena in which they hope to impress seems somehow smaller—the courthouse rather than the city or state. This tempered ambition is ironic, however, in the light of the network television cameras. The media demand that the stereotypes be acted out. It is to their credit that most of the attorneys remain focused on their goals despite this distraction.

What an examination of the trial process in this narrative reveals is that the struggle in the courtroom to interpret events, explain behavior, and assess blame reflects the struggle going on in society at large. Merrill suggests that Mailer's unifying theme is what Mailer has called "American Virtue": "everyone involved here wished to do 'the right thing' and went to some trouble to act accordingly . . . all did their best as they understood the best" (178). The narrative demonstrates, however, that regardless of good intentions everyone is trapped in the legal process which grinds on no matter how "virtuous" one chooses to be. We have come a long way from the America where Dreiser saw an individual punished by the same system that produced his dreams. In Mailer's world, the environment is even more chaotic and inexplicable, and we are all dreamers who have difficulty coping. We cannot go back to the America of Dreiser; unfortunately we must go forward, lacking any greater insight into human behavior than existed in Dreiser's day.

NOTES

1. There is some question about the effects of medication Gary has been given in the past, especially Prolixin. Mailer presents the issue in the form of a dream of Dr. Woods's in which he cross-examines a doctor who prescribes Prolixin, a practice of which Woods disapproves (Mailer 397–98). In his afterword Mailer indicates,

> the cross-examination that John Woods makes of a psychiatrist who administers Prolixin comes in fact from an actual interview by Lawrence Schiller and myself a couple of years later and has been placed in Dr. Woods' mind with his kind permission. (Mailer 1021)

2. The NAACP intervenes in death penalty cases because it believes that the death penalty is constitutionally defective. The argument is that the death penalty has a disproportionate impact on blacks because more blacks than whites receive the death penalty, and this disproportionate impact indicates a violation of the equal protection clause.

CONCLUSION

Our two-tiered examination of the works by Dreiser, Wright, Capote, and Mailer reveals, in the narrower context, the selection process used by each author when choosing the elements of a trial to include in his presentation of a trial scene. The trial scenes in the four narratives are similar in that each writer understands and adheres to the outline of a model trial, and all of the writers provide background information on the attorneys involved in the cases. But the writers do select different aspects of the trial process to emphasize in order to support various themes. For example, Dreiser summarizes jury selection in a few sentences because he wants to move quickly to the opening statements by the lawyers that are an important component of his argument that the system can never provide justice for someone it understands so little about, such as Clyde, while Capote highlights jury selection to emphasize the composition of the jury—all "insiders"—and ignores opening statements because to Capote the reactions of the defendants are more important than the rhetoric of the lawyers.

As another example of the authors' selection process, Dreiser downplays closing arguments because everything has already been said in the opening statements while Wright has his protagonist plead guilty so Wright can highlight the speech of the defense attorney, which contains extra-legal material, in a mitigation hearing.

The second, broader level of our examination concerns whether or not these crimes represent the era in which they occur. This book reveals that the style of presentation, the tone of the scenes, and the kinds of issues addressed do change over the fifty years between

Dreiser's narrative and Mailer's.   Dreiser presents a naturalistic examination of Clyde's thoughts as Clyde moves through the legal system, and Wright depicts the world views of Bigger and Boris Max from an omniscient point of view. The style of Capote and Mailer broadens to the points of view of a larger cast of characters who speak to us in their own voices rather than the voices of the authors. Mailer and Capote step out of the narrative and allow the characters to tell their own stories with minimal authorial interruption.

Not only the style but also the tone of the narratives changes over time. All of the authors show some compassion for the murderers, but the characters themselves respond more rebelliously as the century progresses. Clyde plans an act of rebellion, but Roberta's death is ultimately accidental. Clyde is resigned to his fate at an early stage in the proceedings because he accepts the prevailing morality and knows he must be punished for violating that moral code. Bigger cannot accept the prevailing racist code. He lashes out, however, in fear rather than anger. He accidentally smothers Mary out of fear of punishment by white society. Once in custody, Bigger discovers that owning his act is a way of affirming his identity, of taking his place in a society that offered him limited roles. Perry and Dick defy authority at every turn. The seriousness of their crimes escalates until they commit murder. Gary Gilmore also rebels early, beginning in reform school and ending with the ultimate act of rebellion: challenging the state to execute him.

As society becomes more complicated in the latter half of the twentieth century, so too do the issues explored in these narratives become more complex. Dreiser's text deals with the destructiveness of the American Dream, that is, the social, moral, and legal implications of the pursuit of that dream at all costs. Wright's work deals with the same issues of social and economic stratification and adds the elements of race and political ideology to the discussion. Capote's narrative addresses social issues of isolation and the pervasiveness of evil and focuses on the psychological side of the protagonists.

Everyone wonders why the Clutters had to be shot. Mailer's text includes all of the issues found in Dreiser and Capote plus the subjects of sexuality, psychiatry, institutional and individual religion, and media involvement in the legal process. For example, Dreiser used the newspaper as a source of information while to Mailer the media become a source of disinformation or distortion of personalities and events.

Another pattern in the trial scenes of these authors is worth noting. Although none of the writers paints a particularly flattering picture of the lawyers involved in the judicial process, the lawyers are treated less harshly as we move from Dreiser's politically motivated, self-involved, self-righteous prosecutor and defenders, to Wright's Boris Max, who wants to understand his client, and finally to Mailer's prosecutor, who genuinely admires the defendant and feels it is the system that has failed. Mailer's portrait of the trial attorneys and the appellate attorneys is often sympathetic despite Mailer's personal view of lawyers: " '. . . it's hard to think of a lawyer as being *very* decent . . . ' " (qtd. in Bragg 255). Mailer himself expressed surprise at the sincerity and commitment of the lawyers on all sides of the Gilmore case (Bragg 255; Buckley and Greenfield 239, 240, 250). To Mailer, the lawyers are human; it is the system that is absurd. Of course, one could argue that Mailer has merely substituted the media representatives for the lawyers as objects of his contempt in the narrative.

Perhaps the most striking change that occurs over the half century between *An American Tragedy* and *The Executioner's Song* is the progressive senselessness of the crimes committed. Clyde has a motive: he aspires to Sondra and her wealth and social status, just as, Dreiser points out, any red-blooded American boy would do given the society in which Clyde was raised. Bigger's motive for wanting to keep Mary quiet is not to advance himself but to protect himself. He acts out of fear and to survive in a society that will surely punish him for being in the bedroom of a drunk white woman at 2:00 a.m. We can understand how Bigger's justifiable fear causes him to act to silence Mary, and we can acknowledge, while not condone, the element of self-protection in Bigger's premeditated killing of Bessie. The actions of Perry and Dick are not so understandable. Yes, they have a motive for going to the Clutter house, robbery, but the murder of the four Clutters is unnecessary. Arguably, the family would have had a difficult time ever identifying the men, and all Perry and Dick gain is about forty dollars, a radio, and a pair of binoculars. Gary Gilmore commits the ultimate motiveless crime. There is no evidence that he goes to the gas station or motel to rob. What he steals is incidental to the act of killing his randomly chosen victims. In America in the late 1970s not even an articulate criminal such as Gilmore can explain why he committed these senseless shootings.

> There was no sense or any way you could understand it, except that, as Gilmore said to many people afterwards, he said, "If you want to understand murder, don't look for motive, look to the idea that a person gets so full of rage that they commit murder, that it's a way of opening a valve." And he spoke of his murder in that way, as a matter of venting tension. (Mailer qtd. in Buckley and Greenfield 232)

Left unanswered is the question of the source of all that rage. Are we as a society creating our own monsters? And how are we to judge acts committed to "vent tension"? Foucault points out that we have come to judge more than the crime; now we judge the "soul" of the criminal. As Foucault sees it, "A whole set of assessing, diagnostic, prognostic, normative judgements concerning the criminal have become lodged in the framework of penal judgement."

> The question is no longer simply: "Has the act been established and is it punishable?" But also: "What *is* this act, what *is* this act of violence or this murder? To what level or to what field of reality does it belong? Is it a phantasy, a psychotic reaction, a delusional episode, a perverse action?" It is no longer simply: "Who committed it?" But: "How can we assign the causal process that produced it? Where did it originate in the author himself? Instinct, unconscious, environment, heredity?" It is no longer

simply: "What law punishes the offence?" But: "What would be the most appropriate measures to take? How do we see the future development of the offender? What would be the best way of rehabilitating him?" (Foucault 19)

And still we have no answers. Mills suggests Mailer is describing the changing reality of postwar America as Mailer experienced the change, that he is exploring the contemporary American psyche (432). If Meyer Levin is correct, that certain crimes come to stand for the era in which they occur, the era represented by Gilmore's crime is a bleak one indeed, in which neither the perpetrator nor the victim understands the cause of his or her pain.

Almost two decades have passed since a narrative based on an actual crime by a major American author was published. Dreiser, Wright, Capote, and Mailer carefully chose the cases for their texts. From where might the next such case come? One need look no further than a June evening in Los Angeles in 1994. A beautiful blond and a younger male were stabbed to death that night. Her ex-husband, a famous and wealthy African-American, stands accused of the crime. The case is People v. Orenthal James Simpson, and it vividly demonstrates the thesis that the courtroom is a forum for contemporary social issues.

O. J. Simpson, like Bigger Thomas, is an outsider by race. Unlike Bigger or Clyde Griffiths, however, he is wealthy and has social status based on his fame garnered as a professional athlete. Unlike the defendants in any of the four narratives we reviewed, Simpson has the notoriety to attract, and the financial means to pay for, the best legal talent and scientific expertise available. This is not a situation where the accused is dependent on a public defender, a court-appointed attorney, or an interested organization such as the NAACP which was involved in the actual cases on which *Native Son* and *The Executioner's Song* were based. Simpson has the funds to direct his own defense.

The first victim was Simpson's ex-wife, Nicole Brown, who was the mother of his two bi-racial children. Simpson and Brown had been divorced for several years, and there is evidence of incidents of domestic abuse during the marriage including police reports, recordings of 911 calls, and a diary and photographs left by Brown in a safe deposit box. The second victim, Brown's acquaintance Ron Goldman, was an aspiring model and a waiter at a restaurant frequented by Brown where she and family members ate dinner on the night of the murders. The personal relationship, if any, between the two victims has not been disclosed.

The cultural mix of the characters in this drama make the Simpson trial an excellent example of the courtroom as forum in the last decade of the twentieth century. The diversity reflects the cultural changes in many regions of the United States since the publication of Dreiser's *An American Tragedy* in 1925. Multicultural legal teams were presided over by an Asian-American judge. The original jury, comprised of twelve regular and twelve alternate jurors, was also mixed by race and gender. The witnesses who testified ranged from a chief medical examiner of East-Indian origin to a female screen writer to a mob informant. Represented were not only various races and genders but also a wide array of economic statuses, from a chauffeur and housekeeper to the president of a corporation and the wives of celebrities who were friends of Nicole Brown.

Just as the lawyers in our four narratives were concerned with their reputations and some were politically ambitious, the prosecution and defense attorneys in the Simpson case had their reputations enhanced merely by participating in this nationally televised trial. The attorneys themselves gained celebrity status. They mirrored the ethnic, racial, and gender mix of the other participants in the trial. The prosecution team, led by a white female and a black male, generated questions about the child care responsibilities of working women and the tensions within the growing African-American legal community. The power struggle among the defense attorneys, with

Jewish Robert Shapiro as the architect of the team and African-American Johnnie Cochran as the spokesperson, was highlighted by the media throughout the trial. Once the verdict was rendered, several lawyers retained agents to represent them through the William Morris agency.

Numerous and multifaceted legal issues in the case were raised in the preliminary hearing, in extensive pretrial motions including a motion to suppress evidence gathered during a warrantless search, and at trial. Constitutional issues of First Amendment free speech, Fourth Amendment search and seizure, and Fifth Amendment immunity against self-incrimination were all raised by various participants in the process. No California statute was left unchallenged in defense of Simpson. As Kaminer has noted, "the concern the public showed for procedural rights in the Simpson case was in striking contrast to general disdain for 'criminal's rights' " (34).

Issues of the effect of science and technology on the trial process were also presented in People v. Simpson. Forensic experts battled over the analysis of hair, fibers, blood types, blood spatter patterns, and shoe imprints. Scientific procedures not in existence for, or not involved in, the earlier narratives were displayed here. Questions of the reliability of DNA evidence, for example, have brought a range of DNA experts, both scientific and legal, onto the forum. Technology played a large role in how the trial was administered. Computers were used to catalog and display evidence. Individual attorneys worked from laptop computers in the courtroom. The court reporters created computer-generated transcripts, and the judge had a computer on the bench to review testimony and exhibits. These technological advances arguably alter the course of a trial in many ways and would provide interesting material for use by an author in the future. For instance, there could now be a record of planning strategies between attorneys as they communicate silently by computer during the trial.

Perhaps the technological and cultural feature of the Simpson trial most representative of the 1990s was the television coverage by media outlets such as *CNN* and *Court TV*. The media attention to this "trial of the century" might be compared to the coverage of the Hauptmann trial in the Lindbergh kidnapping case which also received that appellation in the 1930s. The Hauptmann trial was filmed, but that newsreel coverage was not continuous and was not available for viewing in one's home. The Simpson case offered gavel to gavel coverage with commentary from the television networks' legal experts who, as Kaminer points out, "deconstruc[t] every move by the prosecution and defense, just as political pundits deconstruct political campaigns" (35). The television coverage raised many cultural questions, such as the fairness of the television coverage to the defendant and the witnesses, whether the camera alters behavior in the courtroom, and what impact the coverage has on viewers' perceptions of the criminal justice system.

The most highly charged social issue of the Simpson case was that of race. The defense attorneys certainly saw racism in the beliefs and actions of L.A.P.D. detective Mark Fuhrman who was hard pressed to deny his racist comments recorded on tape. Racism was also alleged by the defense in the selection of the black male prosecutor. It is likely that race was one factor considered by both sides in the jury selection process. It could be suggested that by the end of the twentieth century the blatant racism that was accepted and endorsed against Bigger Thomas was now unacceptable, if no less prevalent, in the trial of O. J. Simpson. To be racist in the 1990s is to be branded an outsider, a rogue cop, rather than a member of the majority as was true in Wright's society. One vivid example of the contrasting views of racism in Wright's narrative and the Simpson case is that Wright named his character "Bigger" to remind the reader of the term "nigger" that was being applied to black men while at Simpson's trial it was unacceptable to even speak the "N" word.

The rejection of racist ideology at the same time that racism is used as a defense tactic is ironic. In the racial climate of the 1990s, a black defendant of Simpson's celebrity and wealth could arguably be helped, not hindered, by his race. To convict Simpson would be viewed by some as applying the same racist attitudes prevailing in Wright's America. What this view ignores is the fact that Simpson was represented by black attorneys and judged by a predominantly black jury. Asserting that a conviction of Simpson would be based on his color alone also ignores the physical evidence in the case.

While race was a volatile issue in the case, the economic status of the defendant may have been more of a controlling factor. Simpson had millions to spend in his own defense. Any individual, whether black or white, without resources would have been less likely to prevail. Raising doubt in the minds of jurors is an expensive undertaking in today's legal system.

In order to avoid a conviction, Simpson's attorneys argued that the racist attitudes of the police led to the planting of evidence against their client. Johnnie Cochran's plea in his closing argument that the jurors not become part of the conspiracy is strikingly similar to the sociological issues raised by Max in defense of Bigger Thomas. Cochran's "jury nullification" argument, that the jurors should send a message to the system about police racism and misconduct by acquitting this defendant, however, differs from Max's argument in two ways. Max was arguing for a lesser punishment rather than an acquittal of the crime for which Bigger had already pled guilty, and Cochran's argument was successful.

The recent history of legal decisions in California has demonstrated that California juries are sometimes swayed by sociological principles rather than the principles of law as presented by the judge. Two examples would be the first trials of the Menendez brothers and of the officers accused in the Rodney King beating. The sequestered jury in the Simpson case had an unusually high number of jurors dismissed for conduct or prior activities rather than the usual health reasons, and the jurors were proactive in asserting their rights by "striking" over a change in the juror supervision staff and by engaging in interviews and bookwriting after their dismissal. These were not the Yankee jurors of *An American Tragedy* or the midwesterners of *In Cold Blood*. One might ask, however, how even in California a verdict can be rendered after less than four hours of deliberation when the case has been presented through more than one hundred witnesses and one thousand exhibits over a nine-month period. Was Johnnie Cochran's racist, sociological argument the deciding factor for these jurors? Or were they simply not convinced beyond a reasonable doubt by the evidence presented by the prosecution? Either conclusion would provide fodder for effective narrative.

The verdict has been rendered in the case of People v. O. J. Simpson. Is this trial the stuff of which great narratives are made? At least two writers who have previously authored books based on actual crimes must believe so. Joe McGinniss and Dominick Dunne were assigned regular seats in the courtroom by Judge Ito. What they witnessed became a national referendum on race and the effectiveness and fairness of the judicial process.

This examination of the ways in which authors have represented homicide trials throughout twentieth-century American literature was begun long before the commission of the crime that led to the O. J. Simpson trial. The Simpson case merely serves as a vivid contemporary example of the courtroom as forum for social issues beyond the acquittal or conviction of an individual defendant.

What the law offers to literature is a forum, the courtroom, in which to present important social issues. What literature offers the law is a form, the written word, in which to present the law in a comprehensible manner to a wide audience and to raise important questions about the legal process. The trial scenes by Dreiser, Wright, Capote, and Mailer are effective because they are faithful to both the realities of the forum and the thematic possibilities of the form.

WORKS CITED

Aldridge, John W. "An Interview with Norman Mailer." *Conversations with Norman Mailer*. Ed. J. Michael Lennon. Jackson, MS: UP of Mississippi, 1988. 262–70.

Blake, Caesar. "On Richard Wright's *Native Son*." *Rough Justice: Essays on Crime in Literature*. Ed. M. L. Friedland. Toronto: U of Toronto P, 1991. 187–99.

Blake, Manfred Nelson. "The Volcano of Anger." *Novelists' America: Fiction as History, 1910–1940*. Syracuse: Syracuse UP, 1969. 226–53.

Bone, Robert A. *The Negro Novel in America*. Rev. ed. New Haven: Yale UP, 1965.

Bragg, Melvyn. "A Murderer's Tale: Norman Mailer Talking to Melvyn Bragg." *Conversations with Norman Mailer*. Ed. J. Michael Lennon. Jackson, MS: UP of Mississippi, 1988. 252–61.

Brazil, John R. "Murder Trials, Murder, and Twenties America." *American Quarterly* 33 (Summer 1981): 163–84.

Breen, Jon L. *Novel Verdicts: A Guide to Courtroom Fiction*. Metuchen, NJ: Scarecrow Press, 1984.

Buckley, William F. Jr. and Jeff Greenfield. "Crime and Punishment:
    Gary Gilmore." *Conversations with Norman Mailer.* Ed. J.
    Michael Lennon. Jackson, MS: UP of Mississippi, 1988.
    228–51.

Capote, Truman. *In Cold Blood.* NY: NAL, 1965.

___.   "The Guts of a Butterfly." *Tynan Right and Left: Plays,
    Films, People, Places, and Events.* Kenneth Tynan. NY:
    Atheneum, 1968. 447–452.

Castle, John F. "The Making of *An American Tragedy.*" Diss. U of
    Michigan, 1952.

Christensen, Peter G. "Truman Capote (1924-1984)." *Contemporary
    Gay American Novelists: A Bio-Bibliographical Critical
    Sourcebook.* Ed. Emmanuel S. Nelson. Westport, CT: Green-
    wood, 1993. 46–59.

Clarke, Gerald. *Capote: A Biography.* NY: Simon, 1988.

Cole, George F. *The American System of Criminal Justice.* 4th ed.
    Monterey, CA: Brooks/Cole Publishing Co., 1986.

Collett, Alan.   "Literature, Criticism, and Factual Reporting."
    Philosophy and Literature 13 (Oct. 1989): 282–296.

Cowley, Malcolm. "Richard Wright: The Case of Bigger Thomas."
    20th-Century Interpretations of Native Son. Ed. Houston A.
    Baker, Jr. Englewood Cliffs, NJ: Prentice, 1972. 112–14.

Dreiser, Theodore. *An American Tragedy.* 1925. NY: NAL, 1964.

Dunlop, C. R. B. "Law and Justice in Dreiser's *An American Tragedy.*" *University of British Columbia Law Review* 6 (1971): 379–403.

Dupee, F. W. "Truman Capote's Score." *The New York Review of Books* 6 (Feb. 3, 1966): 3–5.

Edmundson, Mark. "Romantic Self-Creations: Mailer and Gilmore in *The Executioner's Song.*" *Contemporary Literature* 31 (1990): 434–47.

Fabre, Michel. *The Unfinished Quest of Richard Wright.* Trans. Isabel Barzun. NY: William Morrow, 1973.

Fishkin, Shelley Fisher. Epilogue. *From Fact to Fiction: Journalism and Imaginative Writing in America.* Baltimore: Johns Hopkins, 1985. 207–17.

Foucault, Michel. *Discipline and Punish: The Birth of the Prison.* Trans. Alan Sheridan. NY: Pantheon, 1977.

Friedland, M. L. Introduction. *Rough Justice: Essays on Crime in Literature.* Ed. M. L. Friedland. Toronto: U of Toronto P, 1991.

Gallagher, Mary Kathleen. "From Natty to Bigger: The Innocent Criminal in American Fiction." Diss. U of North Carolina at Chapel Hill, 1982. *DAI* 43 (1982): 167-A.

Galloway, David. "Why the Chickens Came Home to Roost in Holcomb, Kansas: Truman Capote's *In Cold Blood.*" *Truman Capote's In Cold Blood: A Critical Handbook.* Ed. Irving Malin. Belmont, CA: Wadsworth, 1968. 154–63.

Garrett, George. "Crime and Punishment in Kansas: Truman Capote's *In Cold Blood.*" *The Hollins Critic* 3 (Feb. 1966): 1–12.

Garvey, John. *"The Executioner's Song."* *Modern Critical Views: Norman Mailer.* Ed. Harold Bloom. NY: Chelsea, 1986. 139–42.

Gaute, J. H. H. and Robin Odell. *The New Murderers' Who's Who.* NY: International Polygonics, Ltd., 1989.

Gerber, Philip. " 'A Beautiful Legal Problem': Albert Lévitt on *An American Tragedy.*" *Papers on Language and Literature* 27 (Spring 1991): 214–42.

Gilmore, Mikal. *Shot in the Heart.* NY: Doubleday, 1994.

Grenander, M. E. "Criminal Responsibility in *Native Son* and *Knock on Any Door.*" *American Literature* 49 (1977): 221–33.

Grobel, Lawrence. *"In Cold Blood."* *Conversations with Capote.* NY: NAL, 1985. 109–27.

Hakutani, Yoshinobu. *"Native Son* and *An American Tragedy:* Two Different Interpretations of Crime and Guilt." *Centennial Review* 23 (1979): 208–26.

Hayne, Barrie. "Dreiser's *An American Tragedy.*" *Rough Justice: Essays on Crime in Literature.* Ed. M. L. Friedland. Toronto: U of Toronto P, 1991. 170–86.

Hellmann, John. "Death and Design in *In Cold Blood:* Capote's 'Nonfiction Novel' as Allegory." *Ball State University Forum* 21 (1980): 65–78.

Hersey, John. "The Legend on the License." *The Yale Review* 70 (Autumn 1980): 1–25.

Hickock, Richard Eugene. "America's Worst Crime in Twenty Years." As Told to Mack Nations. *Male* 11 (Dec. 1961): 30–31, 76–83.

Holladay, Hilary. *"Native Son's* Guilty Man." *The CEA Critic* 54 (Winter 1992): 30–36.

Hollowell, John. "Truman Capote's 'Nonfiction Novel.' " *Fact and Fiction: The New Journalism and the Nonfiction Novel.* Chapel Hill: U of North Carolina P, 1977. 63–86.

Kaminer, Wendy. *It's all the Rage: Crime and Culture.* Reading, MA: Addison-Wesley, 1995.

Kauffmann, Stanley. "Capote in Kansas." *The New Republic* 154 (Jan. 22, 1966): 19–21, 23.

Kinnamon, Keneth. "How *Native Son* Was Born." *Writing the American Classics.* Eds. James Barbour and Tom Quirk. Chapel Hill: U of North Carolina P, 1990. 209–34.

___. *"Native Son." Bigger Thomas.* Ed. Harold Bloom. NY: Chelsea, 1990. 60–72.

___. *"Native Son:* The Personal, Social, and Political Background." *Phylon* (Spring 1969): 66–72.

Levin, Meyer. Foreword. *Compulsion.* 1956. NY: Dell, 1991.

Lingeman, Richard. *Theodore Dreiser: An American Journey 1908–1945*. NY: Putnam's, 1990.

___. *Theodore Dreiser: At the Gates of the City 1871–1907*. NY: Putnam's, 1986.

Mailer, Norman. *The Executioner's Song*. NY: Warner, 1979.

Manso, Peter. *Mailer: His Life and Times*. NY: Simon, 1985.

McAleer, John J. *"An American Tragedy* and *In Cold Blood."* *Thought: A Review of Culture and Idea* 47 (1972): 569–86.

McLaughlin, Robert L. "History vs. Fiction: The Self-Destruction of *The Executioner's Song*." *CLIO* 17 (1988): 225–38.

McWilliams, John P. Jr. "Innocent Criminal or Criminal Innocence: The Trial in American Fiction." *Law and American Literature: A Collection of Essays*. Carl S. Smith, John P. McWilliams, Jr., and Maxwell Bloomfield. NY: Knopf, 1983. 45–124.

Merrill, Robert. *Norman Mailer Revisited*. NY: Twayne, 1992.

Mills, Hilary. *Mailer: A Biography*. NY: Empire, 1982.

Morris, Robert K. "Capote's Imagery." *Truman Capote's* In Cold Blood*: A Critical Handbook*. Ed. Irving Malin. Belmont, CA: Wadsworth, 1968. 176–86.

Nolan, Joseph R. and Jacqueline M. Nolan-Haley. *Black's Law Dictionary*. 6th ed. St. Paul, MN: West, 1990.

Olster, Stacey. "Norman Mailer after Forty Years." *Michigan Quarterly Review* 28 (1989): 400–16.

Pearson, Edmund. *Studies in Murder*. NY: Modern Library, 1938.

Pizer, Donald. *"An American Tragedy."* *Modern Critical Interpretations of Theodore Dreiser's* An American Tragedy. Ed. Harold Bloom. NY: Chelsea, 1988. 45–67.

———. "Documentary Narrative as Art: William Manchester and Truman Capote." *Journal of Modern Literature* 2 (Sept. 1971): 105–18.

Plank, Kathryn M. "Dreiser's Real American Tragedy." *Papers on Language and Literature* 27 (Spring 1991): 268–87.

Plimpton, George. "The Story Behind a Nonfiction Novel." *The New York Times Book Review* (Jan. 16, 1966): 2–3, 38–43.

Posner, Richard A. *Law and Literature: A Misunderstood Relation*. Cambridge, MA: Harvard UP, 1988.

Rampersad, Arnold. Introduction. *Richard Wright: A Collection of Critical Essays*. Ed. Arnold Rampersad. Englewood Cliffs, NJ: Prentice-Hall, 1995. 1–11.

———. Notes. *Richard Wright Early Works:* Lawd Today!, Uncle Tom's Children, Native Son. NY: The Library of America, 1991.

———. "Too Honest for His Own Time." *The New York Times Book Review* (Dec. 29, 1991): 3, 17–18.

Redden, Dorothy S. "Richard Wright and *Native Son*: Not Guilty." *Black American Literature Forum* 10 (1976): 111–16.

Reed, Kenneth T. "The Shift to Reportage." *Truman Capote*. Boston: Twayne, 1981. 94–118.

Reilly, John M. "Giving Bigger a Voice: The Politics of Narrative in *Native Son*." *New Essays on* Native Son. Ed. Keneth Kinnamon. Cambridge: Cambridge UP, 1990. 35–62.

Rollyson, Carl E. Jr. *The Lives of Norman Mailer*. NY: Paragon House, 1991.

____. "Biography in a New Key." *Chicago Review* 31 (1980): 31–38.

Rosenman, Mona G. *"An American Tragedy*: Constitutional Violations." *Dreiser Newsletter* 9 (Spring 1978): 11–19.

Saltzman, Jack. "I Find the Real American Tragedy (by T. Dreiser)." *Resources for American Literary Study* 2 (1972): 3–74.

Schleifer, Ronald. "American Violence: Dreiser, Mailer, and the Nature of Intertextuality." *Intertextuality and Contemporary American Fiction*. Eds. Patrick O'Donnell and Robert Con Davis. Baltimore: Johns Hopkins UP, 1989. 121–43.

Siegel, Paul N. "The Conclusion of Richard Wright's *Native Son*." *Richard Wright: A Collection of Critical Essays*. Eds. Richard Macksey and Frank E. Moorer. Englewood Cliffs, NJ: Prentice, 1984. 106–16.

Smith, Carl S. "Law as Form and Theme in American Letters: An Essay in Law and American Literature." *Law and American Literature: A Collection of Essays*. Carl S. Smith, John P. McWilliams, and Maxwell Bloomfield. NY: Knopf,1983. 1-44

Strychacz, Thomas. "The Plots of Murder: Un/Original Stories in Theodore Dreiser's *An American Tragedy*." *Modernism, Mass Culture, and Professionalism*. Cambridge: Cambridge UP, 1993. 84–116.

Tompkins, Phillip K. "In Cold Fact." *Esquire* 65 (June 1966): 125, 127, 166–71.

Trigg, Sally Day. "Theodore Dreiser and the Criminal Justice System in *An American Tragedy*." *Studies in the Novel* 22 (Winter 1990): 429–440.

Trilling, Diana. "Capote's Crime and Punishment." *Partisan Review* 33 (Spring 1966): 252–59.

Tynan, Kenneth. "The Coldest of Blood." *Tynan Right and Left: Plays, Films, People, Places, and Events*. NY: Atheneum, 1968. 441–46.

Walker, Anne Graffam. "The Verbatim Record: The Myth and the Reality." *Discourse and Institutional Authority: Medicine, Education, and Law*. Eds. Sue Fisher and Alexandra Dundas Todd. Norwood, NJ: Ablex Publishing, 1986. 205–22.

Walker, Margaret. *Richard Wright, Daemonic Genius: A Portrait of the Man and a Critical Look at his Work*. NY: Warner, 1988.

Webb, Constance. *Richard Wright: A Biography*. NY: Putnam, 1968.

Weisberg, Richard. "Law in and as Literature: Self-Generated Meaning in the 'Procedural Novel.' " *The Comparative Perspective on Literature: Approaches to Theory and Practice.* Eds. Clayton Koelb and Susan Noakes. Ithaca: Cornell UP, 1988. 224–32.

West, Rebecca. "A Grave and Reverend Book." *Harper's* 232 (Feb. 1966): 108, 110, 112–14.

White, James Boyd. *Heracles' Bow: Essays on the Rhetoric and Poetics of the Law.* Madison: U of Wisconsin P, 1985.

Wright, Richard. "How 'Bigger' Was Born." *Twentieth Century Interpretations of* Native Son. Ed. Houston A. Baker, Jr. Englewood Cliffs, NJ: Prentice, 1972. 21–47.

___. *Native Son.* 1940. NY: Harper, 1966.

Yurick, Sol. "Sob-Sister Gothic." *The Nation* 202 (Feb. 7, 1966): 158–60.

INDEX